Securing WebLogic Server 12c

Learn to develop, administer, and troubleshoot your WebLogic Server

Luca Masini

Rinaldi Vincenzo

BIRMINGHAM - MUMBAI

Securing WebLogic Server 12c

First published: November 2012

Production Reference: 1201112

Published by Packt Publishing Ltd.
Livery Place
35 Livery Street
Birmingham B3 2PB, UK.

ISBN 978-1-84968-778-2

www.packtpub.com

Credits

Authors
Luca Masini

Rinaldi Vincenzo

Reviewers
Andrea Fiorentini

Michel Schildmeijer

Acquisition Editor
Rukhsana Khambatta

Commissioning Editor
Priyanka Shah

Technical Editor
Dominic Pereira

Copy Editors
Aditya Nair

Alfida Paiva

Project Coordinator
Michelle Quadros

Proofreader
Maria Gould

Indexer
Tejal Daruwale

Production Coordinator
Melwyn D'sa

Cover Work
Melwyn D'sa

Cover Image
Sheetal Aute

About the Authors

Luca Masini is a Senior Software Engineer and Architect who started as a Game Developer for Commodore 64 (Football Manager) and Commodore Amiga (Ken il Guerriero); he soon switched to object-oriented programming and, from its inception in 1995, he was always attracted to the Java language.

He worked on this passion as a consultant for some major Italian banks, developing and integrating major software projects for which he has often taken on the technical leadership role. He adapted Java Enterprise in environments where COBOL was the flagship platform, converting them from mainframe-centric to distributed.

He then shifted his focus to open source, starting from Linux, and then enterprise frameworks, with which he was able to introduce concepts like IoC, ORM, and MVC with minimum impact. He was an early adopter of Spring, Hibernate, Struts, and a whole host of other technologies that in the long run have given his customers a technological advantage and because of which development costs have also lowered.

Lately, however, his attention has been completely directed towards the simplification and standardization of development with Java EE, and for this reason he's now working at the Information and Communications Technology department of a large Italian company to introduce advanced build tools (Maven and Continuous Integration), archetypes of projects, and Agile Development with plain standards.

He has worked on the following books published by Packt Publishing:

- *Google Web Toolkit*
- *Spring Web Flow 2*
- *Spring Persistence with Hibernate*

Dedicated to my skunk
(Dedicato alla mia puzzola)

Vincenzo Rinaldi was born in Milan, Italy, and continues to live and work there. He has over 10 years of experience with system administration in critical contexts, where he contributes with designing, managing, and supporting internal IT infrastructures. He studies and researches many technologies, products, Operating Systems, and custom implementations on a daily basis to meet the business processes. He works with many suppliers, internal teams, and customer services in a mass retail company and coordinates a team to work in the middleware, Operating Systems, and DB stack.

He is an RHCE Certified Engineer and also has great experience in WebLogic setup and administration, generally in the middleware layer.

You can read more about him on his Linkedin profile at `http://www.linkedin.com/in/vincenzorinaldi`.

The first big thanks goes to my pregnant wife Nadia and my son Mattia, they have supported me with their energy. One big thanks to my colleague Luca Masini and all those colleagues who supported me in the writing of this book.

About the Reviewers

Andrea Fiorentini graduated in Multimedia Systems and Telecommunications Engineering from the University of Siena in the year 2003. He attended a course for an internship at the company for which he works since June 2004 as a systems engineer and programmer.

The company for which he works is dedicated to providing services to the cooperative credit banks in Italy. He has a sound knowledge of the Oracle database, Application Server (iAS), WebLogic Server, and Business Intelligence software. He has also finished a training course in Oracle named "Developing Oracle Web Services Using Java Technology".

For the last two years he has been the head of the development team at the company that he works for, which specializes in technology-oriented Java using instruments such as GWT+, GXT, and EJB 3.0.

> Thank you very much Luca Masini for giving me this opportunity. I'm very glad I helped in the writing of this book.

Michel Schildmeijer was born in the Netherlands, in the hot summer of 1966. He has lived his entire life in the capital, Amsterdam. After middle school, he started studying Pharmacy. After 4 years, he had to fulfill his military duty at the Royal Dutch Air force, where he worked in a pharmacy.

After this period, he got a job as a Quality Inspector at a pharmacy company; but after about two years he switched his job for a position in a hospital pharmacy, where he has worked for over 10 years.

In the meantime, he married his wife, Tamara, and had two kids, Marciano and Robin. His personal life wasn't always that easy, as his wife got extremely ill for a brief period and he had to take the entire responsibility of managing his family. Fortunately, he got plenty of support from his parents-in-law, who took great care of his kids.

While on his pharmacy job, around 1994, he got acquainted with the Medical Information System that was taking care of structuring patients' medical history and other information. This was a system running on HP UNIX, a MUMPS SQL database and text-based terminal. He started learning UNIX and MUMPS to give operational support. By then he became very enthusiastic, so he made a job switch and started working for some IT companies. Around the year 2000, he started using Oracle on a big banking application for settlements and clearance. The system was running on Oracle 7, AIX UNIX, BEA WebLogic, and BEA Tuxedo. This was the first time that he had worked with WebLogic. From then on, he gained more and more specialized knowledge in Middleware and Oracle. He has worked on many projects for the same. Around 2006, he started working on several projects for IBM in the Oracle Middleware team, administering, configuring, and tweaking large Oracle Middleware systems with Oracle SOA Suite, Oracle Portal, Oracle HTTP, and many more.

In 2008, he started working for Randstad Holding, and gained more and more expertise in developing the middleware infrastructure around applications. He began research on migrating the Oracle Application Server 10g and SOA Suite 10g to the 11g platform. Around that same period, Oracle acquired BEA.

From working in Brussels for Belgacom — a large Telco company in Belgium — he started his own as an Oracle Fusion Middleware Architect, for AMIS, an IT company specializing in Oracle and JAVA.

His focus was always on developing the infrastructure for many companies and advising them how to migrate or build a new middleware platform based on the latest 11g techniques. He also became an instructor, teaching all the basics of Oracle WebLogic.

For him, the reason to review this book was to get familiar with the new features in WebLogic 12c, because he thinks it's a great product with a lot of new features, especially the new JAVA EE 6 features and the Exalogic optimizations.

Michel is now working for Qualogy as a member of the Exalogic Squad Team.

I would like to thank my wife, Tamara, whose life is sometimes a difficult struggle. I would also like to thank Janny and Steef, who took care of my kids Marciano and Robin. I owe thanks to my great kids too.

www.PacktPub.com

Support files, eBooks, discount offers and more

You might want to visit www.PacktPub.com for support files and downloads related to your book.

Did you know that Packt offers eBook versions of every book published, with PDF and ePub files available? You can upgrade to the eBook version at www.PacktPub.com and as a print book customer, you are entitled to a discount on the eBook copy. Get in touch with us at service@packtpub.com for more details.

At www.PacktPub.com, you can also read a collection of free technical articles, sign up for a range of free newsletters and receive exclusive discounts and offers on Packt books and eBooks.

http://PacktLib.PacktPub.com

Do you need instant solutions to your IT questions? PacktLib is Packt's online digital book library. Here, you can access, read and search across Packt's entire library of books.

Why Subscribe?

- Fully searchable across every book published by Packt
- Copy and paste, print and bookmark content
- On demand and accessible via web browser

Free Access for Packt account holders

If you have an account with Packt at www.PacktPub.com, you can use this to access PacktLib today and view nine entirely free books. Simply use your login credentials for immediate access.

Instant Updates on New Packt Books

Get notified! Find out when new books are published by following @PacktEnterprise on Twitter, or the *Packt Enterprise* Facebook page.

Table of Contents

Preface

Security is a must in a modern Enterprise infrastructure, and WebLogic implements a very complete and complex architecture for configuration and implementation. That is why it is necessary to deeply know technologies, terminologies, and how the security process works between all actors. *Securing WebLogic Server 12c* aims to simplify the complex world of WebLogic Security, helping the reader to implement standard Java EE application security, and configuring it inside WebLogic with clean and simple step-by-step examples. This guide will let you develop and deploy in a production system with the best practices, both from the development world and the operation world. From the concepts of Java EE Security to the development of secure applications, from the configuration of a realm to the setup of Kerberos Single Sign-on, every concept is expressed in simple terms and completed by working examples and pictures. Finally, a way to develop WebLogic security providers with Maven is provided, so that you can add the security part of your infrastructure to your enterprise best practices.

What this book covers

Chapter 1, WebLogic Security Concepts, covers the custom concepts and framework that implement security inside the WebLogic server.

Chapter 2, WebLogic Security Realm, will allow you to understand in detail how the internal LDAP works and also explain the necessary configuration. Also explained in this chapter is how an existing LDAP server can be integrated with WebLogic. This chapter includes a complete troubleshooting section that will help you overcome some typical configuration mistakes.

Chapter 3, Java EE Security with WebLogic, explains how you can leverage all the power of WebLogic security using only standard Java EE coding and vice versa. Also, this chapter explains how you can have the value added feature from WebLogic in a standard Java EE application.

Chapter 4, Creating Custom Authentication Providers with Maven, shows a better way to create your own provider that can use the WebLogic framework to integrate your custom security needs.

Chapter 5, Integrating with Kerberos SPNEGO Identity Assertion, covers the Single Sign-On activation process between your Active Directory Domain/Kerberos Server and desktop clients through WebLogic, to access the protected application resource in a seamless way. Every configuration is explained in full detail for this complex task.

What you need for this book

The following are the software that you need for this book:

- WebLogic Server 12c (http://www.oracle.com/technetwork/middleware/fusion-middleware/downloads/index.html)
- Maven (maven.apache.org)
- Java 7 SDK (java.com)

Who this book is for

If you are a WebLogic Server administrator who is looking forward to a step-by-step guide to administer and configure WebLogic security, then this guide is for you. This book is also for WebLogic developers who want to leverage the complex but powerful WebLogic security infrastructure.

Working knowledge of WebLogic and/or Java EE 6 is required.

Conventions

In this book, you will find a number of styles of text that distinguish between different kinds of information. Here are some examples of these styles, and an explanation of their meaning.

Code words in text are shown as follows: "We can also disable the standard maven-install-plugin plugin".

A block of code is set as follows:

```
<plugin>
    <artifactId>maven-compiler-plugin</artifactId>
    <version>2.0.2</version>
```

```
<configuration>
    <encoding>UTF-8</encoding>
    <source>${maven.compiler.source}</source>
    <target>${maven.compiler.target}</target>
</configuration>
</plugin>
<plugin>
```

> Warnings or important notes appear in a box like this.

> Tips and tricks appear like this.

Reader feedback

Feedback from our readers is always welcome. Let us know what you think about this book—what you liked or may have disliked. Reader feedback is important for us to develop titles that you really get the most out of.

To send us general feedback, simply send an e-mail to feedback@packtpub.com, and mention the book title via the subject of your message.

If there is a topic that you have expertise in and you are interested in either writing or contributing to a book, see our author guide on www.packtpub.com/authors.

Customer support

Now that you are the proud owner of a Packt book, we have a number of things to help you to get the most from your purchase.

Downloading the example code

You can download the example code files for all Packt books you have purchased from your account at http://www.PacktPub.com. If you purchased this book elsewhere, you can visit http://www.PacktPub.com/support and register to have the files e-mailed directly to you.

Errata

Although we have taken every care to ensure the accuracy of our content, mistakes do happen. If you find a mistake in one of our books—maybe a mistake in the text or the code—we would be grateful if you would report this to us. By doing so, you can save other readers from frustration and help us improve subsequent versions of this book. If you find any errata, please report them by visiting http://www.packtpub.com/support, selecting your book, clicking on the **errata submission form** link, and entering the details of your errata. Once your errata are verified, your submission will be accepted and the errata will be uploaded on our website, or added to any list of existing errata, under the Errata section of that title. Any existing errata can be viewed by selecting your title from http://www.packtpub.com/support.

Piracy

Piracy of copyright material on the Internet is an ongoing problem across all media. At Packt, we take the protection of our copyright and licenses very seriously. If you come across any illegal copies of our works, in any form, on the Internet, please provide us with the location address or website name immediately so that we can pursue a remedy.

Please contact us at copyright@packtpub.com with a link to the suspected pirated material.

We appreciate your help in protecting our authors, and our ability to bring you valuable content.

Questions

You can contact us at questions@packtpub.com if you are having a problem with any aspect of the book, and we will do our best to address it.

1
WebLogic Security Concepts

Security is a complex matter, and Java EE is not an exception to this rule. To make things even more complicated, WebLogic extends standard security with some important and useful features that will be explored in this chapter; they are as follows:

- Identity Assertion
- Credential Mappers
- **Java Authentication Service Provider Interface for Containers (JASPIC)** and **Java Authentication and Authorization Service (JAAS)**

General concept of security in Java EE

Java standard security is implemented with the security manager and policy files, and is extended by the Java Enterprise Edition in a completely transparent way for the developer; like every other service offered by the platform.

If you are an Enterprise Bean developer, you can develop knowing that the container will take care of the sensitive task of securing your data in the same way it takes care of remoting, translating from HTTP protocol to servlet method call, and transaction management. Obviously, it is impossible for the container to be aware of the infrastructure in which it will be deployed, so there are a lot of standard ways to extend it in order to let it work with a new RDBMS: installing the **Java Database Connectivity (JDBC)** driver JAR files or a new transactional resource that implements the resource adapter contract.

This principle applies to security as well; but until Java EE 6 there were no standard methods of implementing a new Authentication Provider, or whatever is inherent to security. As we'll see, this new version makes it mandatory that containers implement JASPIC 1.0, but many of them implement it in parallel and WebLogic 12c is no exception. If you need to implement something that is not "simple", custom Providers with custom API are required.

In Java EE, the developer interacts with the container using declarative annotations or XML descriptors. When you need to secure a URL managed by a servlet, all you need to do is annotate that servlet with the `@ServletSecurity` annotation along with a list of allowed roles, as shown in the following code snippet:

```
@WebServlet("/mysecuredurl")
@ServletSecurity(@HttpConstraint(rolesAllowed={"myrole"}))
public class MySecuredServlet extends HttpServlet {
    ...
}
```

This single line of meta-code opens up the magic world of Java EE security, as explained in the following points:

- If the user is not authenticated, the web container will ask him/her for his/her credentials; how the user will be asked depends on the configuration of the web application and the kind of client the user is using.

- The user agent accepts the credentials and sends that information to the server. The server then tries to validate them using an Authentication Provider. If this is successful, a suitable container for user principals will be created (a Subject), and this will be mapped to the authenticating agent using a sort of session cookie.

- Once the user principals are known, they are mapped to the application roles that are declared on the custom deployment descriptors of your application server.

- If the servlet needs additional resources or needs to make a call to an EJB method, the security context will be "propagated" (see Java EE 6 specs, v.3.2, at `http://www.oracle.com/technetwork/java/javaee/tech/index.html`).

Every single step described here involves a bunch of very complex tasks, and all of them are free for the Java EE developer; they are made behind the curtain by the container.

WebLogic security architecture

WebLogic security architecture is based on a set of classes in the `weblogic.security.*` package in the **WebLogic Security Framework (WSF)**, which are used to develop Security Providers that run under the auspices of WebLogic Security Service.

This runtime is the orchestrator that allows application components such as EJBs and servlets to communicate with server resources, with the intermediation of the Security Provider.

Here, we will review some basic concepts of WSF that we need to understand to develop custom providers.

Identifying – Subjects, Principals, and Credentials

WebLogic follows the JAAS architecture of Java SE for its security infrastructure: Subjects, Principals, and Credentials. These are explained as follows:

- **Subject**: Information related to the entity that is requesting the secured resources, such as identities (principal) or attributes (credentials)
- **Principal**: Identity associated with the authenticated entity, such as its full name, the username, a **Lightweight Directory Access Protocol (LDAP)** group, and everything that identifies it
- **Credentials**: Attributes related to the entity that is authenticated; they may be security-related, such as a **Kerberos** ticket (`sun.security.krb5.Credentials`) or not security-related, such as attributes that are used by the application

In JAAS, when the `login()` method is called on the current `LoginContext` class, a new `Subject` object is created and the configured `LoginModule` is called in sequence to enrich that object with principals.

So, for instance, it is possible to configure a `LoginModule` interface that adds Kerberos credentials, another `LoginModule`, like WebLogic's `UsernamePasswordLoginModule`, that adds `PasswordCredential`. These are then used by WebLogic to access restricted resources.

WebLogic resources

Java EE 6 defines the security of components such as an EJB or a connection to an **Enterprise Information System (EIS)**; WebLogic resources extend this level of security. The following is a quote defining resources from the official WebLogic 12c documentation:

> *A structured object used to represent an underlying WebLogic Server entity that can be protected from unauthorized access.*

This means that a `DataSource` object can't be accessed directly but only through a `JDBCResource` object, and every resource is also represented as a hierarchy; if security is not specified for the leaf, its single parent can be inspected until a suitable configuration is found.

Suppose, for example, the container is checking if the user is allowed to access a certain method of an EJB, whose resource representation is as follows:

```
type=<ejb>, app=SecuredApp, module=EJBModule, ejb=VeryImportantEJB,
method=callItSecure, methodInterface=Home, methodParams={String, int}
```

If the `EJBResource` class can't find a suitable policy for that method, it will ask its parent, the Enterprise Bean, which can verify if the user is allowed or not.

Writing custom providers – MBeans

Java Management Extensions (JMX) is a mandatory part of the Java EE 6 specification that defines standards for the monitoring and management of Enterprise applications in a dynamic and nonintrusive way. Using JMX, it is possible to query an arbitrary application for diagnostic information without knowing anything about the way it is being implemented, but only using a standard tool like JConsole or VisualVM. This is implemented in a structured way, where JMX defines the runtime, the way Management Beans are developed, and how to access that information. Implementation is straightforward; you only need to define what you want to, as follows:

```
@MXBean
public interface MyManagedProperties {
    public int getCached();
    public void callOperation();
}
```

And the implementation—in Java EE 6 it's really a few lines of code—is as follows:

```
@Singleton
@Startup
public class MyManagedPropertiesBean implements MyManagedProperties {
    private MBeanServer platformMBeanServer;
    private ObjectName objectName = null;
    @PostConstruct
    public void registerInJMX() {
        try {
            objectName = new ObjectName("MyMXBean :type=" + this.
getClass().getName());
            InitialContext ctx = new InitialContext();
            platformMBeanServer = (MBeanServer) ctx.lookup("java:comp/env/
jmx/runtime");
            ctx.close();
            platformMBeanServer.registerMBean(this, objectName);
            } catch (Exception e) {
            throw new IllegalStateException("Problem during registration
of Monitoring into JMX:" + e);
        }
    }
    public int getCached() {//doSomething}
    public void callOperation() {//doSomething}

    @PreDestroy
    public void unregisterFromJMX() {
        try {
            platformMBeanServer.unregisterMBean(this.objectName);
            } catch (Exception e) {
            throw new IllegalStateException("Problem during unregistration
of Monitoring into JMX:" + e);
        }
    }
}
```

An `MXBean` interface is implemented in the previous code; it is a Managed Bean that can be accessed by a JMX client, which doesn't need to know anything about our application. It is the duty of the agent to convert every domain-specific class to simple properties.

Unfortunately, developing MBeans for WebLogic is not that easy, because of a custom way to generate the MBeans that execute in the `MBeanServer` interface. It is necessary to write a custom XML file, called **MBean Definition File (MDF)**, and then generate a JAR file that can be installed on the WebLogic server using WebLogic's MBeanMaker tool.

Authentication Providers

Developing an Authentication Provider is a fairly complex task with many concepts that need to be understood. Here, we will introduce the concepts regarding the composing parts of a provider and different kinds of authentication.

Authentication under WebLogic

Authentication is completely delegated to entities called Authentication Providers, which are a set of classes and configuration files that incorporate an MBean and a `LoginModule` interface. Every time you request a protected resource, every configured Provider is requested to add the principals extracted from the credentials provided.

This mechanism is very similar to the one configurable on the client with only JAAS (and `jaas.config`); the main difference is that it's done with the administration console. This console allows us to configure parameters visually, through the automatically-generated JSP page, without touching any XML file, as shown in the following screenshot:

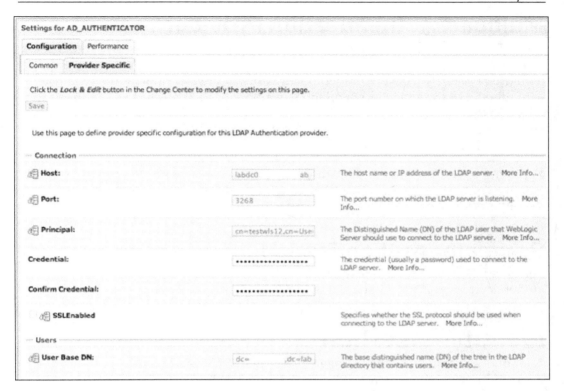

MBean and JAAS

Under WebLogic Security Framework, everything is wrapped by MBeans. The standard JAAS security infrastructure is created and invoked using an MBean, which can be configured using the standard console. This makes sense because the console and every utility that runs under the WebLogic ecosystem has to be consistent and there are a lot of technologies around Java that have to be integrated.

So, if you need to implement your own `LoginModule` interface, remember that you need to "decorate" it with the correct MBean, which in turn is automatically generated for you by the WebLogic MBeanMaker tool.

Multipart Authentication Provider

Every Provider has only one chance to contribute to the authentication process: it receives Credentials and eventually adds Principals to the current Subject. This scenario of security has very limited potentialities if interaction with the user agent is required. For example, for negotiating an authentication mechanism, redirecting to a remote login site, or even implementing a challenge/response handshake, this is a suitable task for servlet filters, but if they are configured for a protected resource they are not called until you are authenticated.

WebLogic Security Framework gives developers a chance to return an array of filters that are executed on behalf of the standard Authentication mechanism, but not under the application component's security context.

Perimeter Authentication

Perimeter Authentication usually uses Identity Assertion and security filters to authenticate users. This will be elaborated later.

Identity Assertion

A lot of organizations have heterogeneous systems that need security services, and many of these systems interact with users that have already declared who they are, for example, during the login phase of their workstation at the beginning of their working day.

This is the basis to introduce the concept of a Perimeter, where authentication is made once and then always trusted during the day. The same happens when you use your badge to enter into your company; you are trusted to be allowed into the buildings, with the need to expose the badge to express that you are an employee. In case of Perimeter Authentication, a token released by a third party is used to extract who the user is, by performing an Identity Assertion and not full authentication.

This means that when developing `LoginModule` interfaces for Identity Assertion providers, Credentials are used not to decide if the user is authenticated, but simply to populate the Subject with the Principals that can be found using the token.

Credential Mapper

Prior to Java EE 6 and the introduction of the `SecurityContext` interface in **Java EE Connector Architecture (JCA)** 1.6 specification (see the `SecurityContext` interface in JCA 1.6 specifications at `http://jcp.org/en/jsr/detail?id=322`), there were no standard ways to map the current `SecurityContext` security object to the `ConnectionSpec` interface of a resource adapter.

This could mean the following two things:

- No end-to-end Single Sign-On from the user to the EIS
- Code into application components that implement mapping of credentials

WebLogic Security Framework supports the mapping of credentials from the current authenticated user to a format that can be understood by the resource adapter/EIS.

The implementation is really straightforward. Before calling the `execute()` method on the interaction in the `ConnectionSpec` interface, the Mapper is asked to convert the current Credentials stored into the Subject into one or more Credentials valid for the remote system.

Currently, if `BasicPassword` is the current authentication mechanism type and `PasswordCredential` is the interface that has to be used for the communication, it's sufficient for the developer of the custom Credentials Mapping provider to write a function that maps the local security space to that of the called EIS.

Conceptually, this is not much different from what is done with Identity Assertion and Perimeter Authentication; but this time the trust is between WebLogic and an external system, with the former responsible for security. Of course, there may also be Mappings that are able to make full authentication, but in both cases the weak link is the Java Application Server that has the chance to authenticate users to a remote system.

JASPIC and Java EE

After so many pages talking about security and how to implement it in WebLogic, the question is: why is all this custom-made and not regulated by Java EE?

Java EE 6 has the correct answer to this question: the JASPIC 1.0 specification, a message processing framework that is protocol-independent and that can do what an Authentication Provider does for us; that is, populate Subjects with Principals and therefore authenticate a remote user agent.

In a manner that is different from WebLogic Security Framework, where everything is inside a secure framework API because the message and the protocol are managed by the application server, this is done at the message level. In this way, it enforces the concept that security is something related to the protocol and the way information is exchanged.

In fact, currently we have three profiles that are part of the standard specification, one that is able to authenticate HTTP clients, another that works with SOAP messages, and a third profile that tries to bridge the new specification with the existing JAAS login module on the market.

This is the first implementation in WebLogic and its immaturity is apparent from the total lack of documentation and the fact that the configuration is not integrated into the custom deployment descriptors. So, consider using it only on noncritical systems.

JACC

Java Authorization Contract for Containers (JACC) is an extension of the standard policy-based security of the JVM for role mapping and authorization of servlets and EJBs. The working of this policy-based security is shown in the following screenshot:

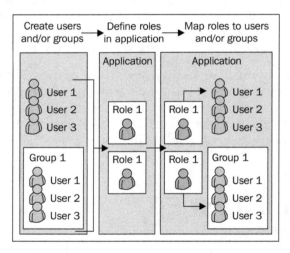

Although it is implemented by WebLogic, Oracle itself discourages its use because of the lack of features and flexibility compared to custom providers, and also because of performance issues. For these reasons, JACC will not be covered in this book.

Summary

This chapter was a quick introduction to WebLogic security fundamentals learning theory that will be used later when a custom provider will be developed or configured inside our domain using the WebLogic console.

It started from Java EE security and then declined to the WebLogic Security Framework, from MBeans to resources.

Finally, two **Java Specification Requests (JSR)** specs were covered, JASPIC and JACC, to show how limited they are compared to custom providers.

2
WebLogic Security Realm

WebLogic security configuration can be difficult to understand. This chapter clearly covers every aspect you need to consider for activating an internal or external user and group structure. Here, you can also find a very useful section about errors and debugging tips, needed to resolve your configuration issues. This chapter includes the following:

- Configuration of local LDAP server: user/roles/lockout
- Configuring an external LDAP for Authentication/Authorization
- Using Identity Assertion

Configuration of local LDAP server: user/roles/lockout

The simplest way to configure your security realm is through the WebLogic Administration Console; you can find all about security in the section, on the main tree, **Security Realms**, where the default configuration called **myrealm** is placed.

Under **Security Realms**, we have a preconfigured subset of Users, Groups, Authentication methods, Role Mapping, Credential Mapping providers, and some other security settings.

You can configure many realms' security sets, but only one will be active.

On the **myrealm** section, we find all security parameters of the internal LDAP server configurations, including users and groups.

Consider this; Oracle declares that the embedded WebLogic LDAP server works well with less than 10,000 users; for more users, consider using a different LDAP server and Authentication Provider, for example, an Active Directory Server.

Users and groups

Obviously, here you can add and configure some internal users and some internal groups. A **user** is an entity that can be authenticated and used to protect our application resources. A **group** is an aggregation of users who usually have something in common, such as a subset of permissions and authorizations.

Users section

The console path for the **Users** section is as follows:

Click on **Security Realms | myrealm | Users and Groups | Users**.

In this section, by default you will find your administrator account, used to log in to the WebLogic Administration Console and configured on the wizard during the installation phase; you can also create some other users (note: the names are case insensitive insert) and set the following settings:

- **User Description**: An internal string description tag
- **User Password**: User password subjected to some rules
- **View User Attributes**: Some user attributes
- **Associate groups**: Predefined in the **Groups** section

Please be attentive to preserve the integrity of the administrative user created in the installation configuration wizard; this user is vital for the WebLogic Server (startup process); don't remove this user if you don't have some advanced knowledge of what you are doing and how to roll back changes.

Take care also to change the admin user's password after installation phase; if you use the automatic startup process without providing a user and password (required when needed to start the admin console in the OS as a service, without prompting any interactive request) you will need to reconfigure the credentials file to start up the admin server at boot. The following file needs to be changed:

```
$DOMAIN_HOME\servers\Adminserver\security\boot.properties
username=weblogic
password=weblogicpassword
```

 After the first boot, the WebLogic admin server will encrypt this file with its internal encryption method.

Groups section

The console path for the **Groups** section is as follows:

Security Realms | myrealm | Users and Groups | Groups

In this section, by default, you will find some groups used to profile user grants (only the Administrators' and Oracle System's group was populated) whose names are case insensitive. Define new groups before creating a user to associate with them. The most important groups are as follows:

- **Administrators**: This is the most powerful group, which can do everything in the WebLogic environment. Do not add plenty of people to it, otherwise you will have too many users with the power to modify your server configuration.

- **Deployers**: This group can manage applications and resources (for example, JDBC, web services) and is very appropriate for the operations team that needs to deploy and update different versions of applications often during the day.

- **Monitors**: This group provides a read-only access to WebLogic and is convenient for monitoring WebLogic resources and status.

- **Operators**: This group provides the grant privilege to stop, start, and resume WebLogic nodes.

All users without an associated group are recognized to an **Anonymous** role. In this case the implicit group (not present in the list) will be the **everyone** group.

Security role condition

The console path for **Roles** and **Policies** are as follows:

- Go to **Security Realms | myrealm | Users and Groups | Realm Roles | Realm Policies | Roles**

- Go to **Security Realms | myrealm | Users and Groups | Realm Roles | Realm Policies | Policies**

In WebLogic, you can configure some advanced collection of rules to trust or deny the access over role security configuration dynamically; all conditions need to be true if you want to grant a security role.

There are some available conditions in WebLogic role mapping, which we will now explore in the next section..

Basic

The available options are as follows:

- **User**: This option adds the user to a specific role if his username matches the specified string
- **Group**: This option adds the specified group to the role in the same way as the previous rule
- **Server is in development mode**: This option adds the user or group in a role if the server is started in the development mode
- **Allow access to everyone**: This option adds all users and groups to the role
- **Deny access to everyone**: This option rejects all users from being in the role

Date and time-based

When used, this role condition can configure a rule based on a date or on a time basis (between, after, before, and specified) to grant a role assignment.

Context element

The server retrieves information from the `ContextHandler` object and allows you to define role conditions based on the values of HTTP servlet request attributes, HTTP session attributes, and EJB method parameters.

User lockout

The console path for **User Lockout** is **Security Realms | myrealm | User Lockout**.

User Lockout is enabled by default; this process prevents user intrusion and dictionary attacks. It also improves the server security and can configure some policies to lock our local configured users. This option is globally applied to any configured security provider.

In this section, you can define the maximum number of consecutive invalid login attempts that can occur before a user's account is locked out and how long the lock lasts. After that period, the account is automatically re-enabled.

If you are using an Authentication Provider that has its own mechanism for protecting user accounts, disable the **Lockout Enabled** option.

When a user is locked, you can find a message similar to the following message in the server logs:

```
<Apr 6, 2012 11:10:00 AM CEST> <Notice> <Security> <BEA-090078> <User
Test in security realm myrealm has had 5 invalid login attempts,
locking account for 30 minutes.>
```

Unlocking user

The result of lock settings are a blocked user; if you need to unlock him immediately, you have to go to the section named **Domain**, created in the wizard installation phase in the left pane under the **Security** section. Here, you can view the **Unlock User** tab, where you can specify that the username be re-enabled. Remember to click on the **Lock & Edit** button before you do any changes.

When you manually unlock a user, you can find a message similar to the following message in the server logs:

```
.... <1333703687507> <BEA-090022> <Explicitly unlocked, user Test.>
```

You can read a sample application configuration to protect your resource and test the previous steps in the *Security in Java EE* section described in the next chapter of this book.

Configuring an external LDAP for Authentication/Authorization

WebLogic supports several types of external authentication providers. Any LDAP v2 or v3 compliant LDAP server should work. Next, we cover the configuration of the Microsoft Active Directory provider in detail, to provide us also with the support for Kerberos **Single Sign-On** (**SSO**) integration in a Microsoft domain network; we will see this in *Chapter 5, Integrating with Kerberos SPNEGO Identity Assertion*.

There are lots of advantages by connecting an existent **Users** and **Groups** infrastructure. It permits us to centralize any object (**Users** and **Groups**) and centrally manage the security rules and policies without the need to access the WebLogic server. Also, any change applied on Active Directory is logically and dynamically propagated to WebLogic security.

To configure our provider faster and easier, we can use the WebLogic console (advanced users can also use the **WebLogic Scripting Tool (WLST)** to make many configuration changes) with an administrative user. Go to the **Security Realms** menu and click on **Providers**. Now we need some important information, which is as follows:

- LDAP Authentication Provider type
- Provider-specific configuration attributes of the LDAP Authentication Provider
- Review performance options that control the cache

 Plan any changes at configuration time in a production environment, because it needs server and Admin server restarts.

Configuring a new provider

The console path for **Providers** is **Security Realms | myrealm | Providers**.

Click on the **Lock & Edit** button, proceed to the **New** button, naming your provider with a personal reference, select the type as **LDAPAuthenticator** and click on **OK**.

More important is the order of providers; WebLogic Security Framework supports more than one Authentication Provider for multipart authentication.

The Authentication Providers need to be arranged in the order in which they will be called; it is important to plan the correct sequence in the login process, the first one starting at the top. You need to use the **Reorder** button to do it.

I advise you to leave the default providers as they are. In this way, you separate and preserve the internal groups and users, most importantly the WebLogic administrator, and you start managing WebLogic without any external providers (think about some connectivity issues to the LDAP/Active Directory server). Afterwards, mapping internal groups to external groups becomes an easy task.

You need to create the same group name in the external provider and associate the external users to it. For this rule, remember that the Active Directory Server also has a default group called **Administrators**; these users will be automatically grouped as WebLogic **Administrators** when the provider is configured.

Control Flag

The console path to work with the **Control Flag** parameter is **Security Realms | myrealm | Providers | Authentication**. Another important parameter present in all authenticator is the **Control Flag** parameter. It establishes how the login sequence uses the Authentication Provider. Using it, we can tweak the security flow process. The available options are as follows:

- **REQUIRED**: This setting establishes that the provider will always be used; the user needs to be checked in order to obtain a trusted access. In any case the authentication continues to follow down to the other providers in the list.

- **REQUISITE**: This setting establishes that the user must pass the provider check in order to be granted access, after that, subsequent providers will be executed.

- **SUFFICIENT**: This setting establishes that the provider does not require the user to pass its check. If it fails, the next provider in the list will be consulted. If the authentication succeeds, no other providers will be used.

- **OPTIONAL**: This setting establishes that the provider's check can be passed or not. If all providers are configured to **OPTIONAL**, the user needs to pass the authentication phase in one of that.

In our scenario, we need to configure one provider connected to Active Directory and leave the default provider, reorder the most-used provider on top, (in our case Active Directory) and switch to **SUFFICIENT** all the provider control flags, as shown in the following diagram:

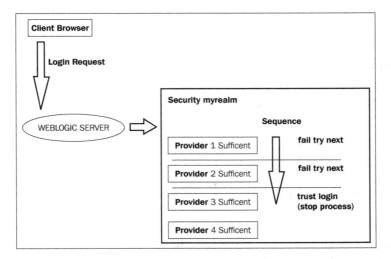

Active Directory provider-specific configuration

Obviously, to configure this provider, we need to have an Active Directory domain structure configured with some groups and users, and know some specific attributes of any customization about your internal LDAP.

Let's start to review the parameters in detail.

Connection

A detailed explanation of the connection parameters are as follows:

- **Host**: Here, you need to specify one or more Active Directory server; the list separator is a blank space. In a production environment, it is a good choice to specify more than one server for high availability. If some host has a different listening port, specify that in the list, otherwise the port specified in the next field will be used. For example, `test.directory.int:1090 test2.directory.int:1091 test3.directory.int`.

- **Port**: Here, you need to specify the Global Catalog TCP/IP listening port (default `3268`).

- **Principal**: Here, you need to specify a valid Active Directory base. The user can connect to Global Catalog and make an LDAP query. We need to specify a correct **Distinguished Name** (**DN**) of the LDAP user. Suppose we have a `EXAMPLEDOM.INT\Users\tecnicalusr` LDAP user, we use `cn=tecnicalusr, cn=Users, dc=exampledom, dc=int`. Remember, the pre-configured folders in the Active Directory are defined as `cn` (for example, **Users**), the custom folders objects will be `ou` in your principal definition path.

- **Credential**: Principal user password used to connect to the LDAP server.

- **SSLEnabled**: Specifies whether an encrypted SSL channel will be used to connect to an LDAP Server. This depends on your Active Directory configuration.

Users

The parameters for **Users** are as follows:

- **User Base DN**: Here, you specify the base distinguished name, where our users and groups are located in the Active Directory tree. You can configure the complete tree of Active Directory or a **subtree**, considering an improved performance while performing search, to dedicate a **subtree** with a small subset of users and groups. For example, `dc=exampledom, dc=int`.

- **User From Name Filter**: Here, you specify the correct filter to search Active Directory users; the default Active Directory configuration can report this query as `(&(sAMAccountName=%u)(objectclass=user))`

- **User Search Scope**: Here, you can select **subtree**—by choosing this option, the query can navigate on **subtree** Active Directory levels. It is a good choice, if your configuration doesn't have a dedicated level and you need to cut down some of the trees.

- **onelevel**: In this case, the query ends on the Active Directory level specified on **User Base DN**.

Groups

The parameters for the **Groups** tab are as follows:

- **Group Base DN**: Here, you specify the base distinguished name on the same lines as that of **User Base DN** and in which level the LDAP query starts for finding the groups. For example, `dc=exampledom, dc=int`.

- **Group From Name Filter**: Here, you specify the filter to search Active Directory groups; the default Active Directory configuration reports the query as `(&(cn=%g)(objectclass=group))`.

- **Group Search Scope**: In the same way as the **User** setting, you can define if the query falls down to **subtree** or stays on the tree specified in the **Group Base DN** parameter.

- **Group Membership Searching**: Here, you can select the group searching options. Limited as well as unlimited searches can be made in the groups using this setting.

- **Max Group Membership Search Level**: If, in the previous parameter, you have selected the **limited** option, here you can specify how many nested user groups follow. If you specify `0`, only the direct membership group will be found. If you specify any positive number, for example, `1`, WebLogic will be able to find the first group membership and the second group inclusion level.

Static groups

The parameters for Static groups are as follows:

- **Static Group Name Attribute**: In the Active Directory, you need to set this parameter to `cn`

- **Static Group Object Class**: In the Active Directory, you need to set this parameter to `group`

- **Static Member DN Attribute**: In the Active Directory, you need to set this parameter to `member`

- **Static Group DNs from Member DN Filter**: These search filters, which extract the distinguished name of a member of a group, return the distinguished name of the static LDAP groups that contain that member, and set this as `(&(member=%M)(objectclass=group))`

General

The General parameters section is as follows:

- **Connection Pool Size**: To start with, we can leave the default value as it is. Subsequently, we can tune this parameter if the single queries take a lot of time and the pool will be exhausted.

- **Connect Timeout**: Here, specify the maximum time in seconds to wait for, until the connection to the LDAP server is established.

  I recommend you to specify the number of seconds; if you set this parameter to `0`, no time limits will be set and you can incur a slowdown in performance and a potential stuck thread problem. Another important aspect of impacting `0` seconds configuration is if you have a list of Active Directory servers, this will not be used because the process is still awaiting a response from the first server in the list. For a good failover, the time is well set between `10-15` seconds in a production environment where more than one Active Directory servers don't increase this number too high. If this timeout is low, you can improve the performance of the login authentication phase in case of an Active Directory failure; this permits us to balance the second Active Directory node in the list.

- **Connection Retry Limit**: This number specifies the total attempts to be made to connect to the LDAP server if the first connection failed. Increase this number to a higher value if you have a single Active Directory server, otherwise set this parameter to a lower value, `1` to switch fast to the second backup Active Directory server; in this way the user login phase can't still wait on the browser side and avoid a timeout issue.

- **Parallel Connect Delay**: This parameter specifies the delay in seconds between concurrent connection attempts to multiple LDAP servers; set this parameter to one or more to create connections in parallel, and not serialized if you have an Active Directory failover list.

- **Results Time Limit**: This parameter specifies the maximum number of milliseconds for the LDAP server to wait for results before a timeout error is raised. If you specify 0, no timeout occurs; configure 0 only if you have more than one Active Directory server and some parallel connections, otherwise consider setting up some seconds after a query times out, to avoid a stuck thread problem in a waiting query response.

- **Cache Enabled**: This parameter enables or disables an internal WebLogic cache LDAP flag to improve your performance.

- **Cache Size**: This parameter defines the size of the cache in KB. Increase this size if you have large Active Directory structure objects and some free WebLogic server resources.

- **Cache TTL**: This parameter specifies how long the internal cache will be flushed and reloaded. Oracle recommends a value of 6000. Consider tuning this value, according to the dynamicity of your Active directory user and group configurations.

- **GUID Attribute**: This parameter specifies the name of the GroupID attribute defined in the Active Directory; the default value is objectguid.

Leave any other setting to the default value or customize it if you have any specific requirement. Now, remember to save any changes made if you have configured your WebLogic installation in production mode. Apply these changes with the green flag button and restart all the servers and also the Admin Server.

After startup, go to **Security Realms | myrealm | Users and Groups** and check if users and groups are configured in your Active Directory server, otherwise check your WebLogic Admin Server logfile and jump to the *Troubleshooting problems* section.

If you have too many results in the list, you can filter on top of the table using the **Customize this table** link. Here, you can insert a filter using a filtering criteria text string or search using a query such as username*. You can also specify the number of rows displayed per page.

Performance options

The console path to work with the **Performance** option is **Security Realms | myrealm | Providers | MyProvider | Performance**.

In this section, you can tune some parameters according to your Active Directory users and groups' hierarchy dimensions. The **Hierarchy Caching** option can improve the server performances; disable this function only if you have poor WebLogic server system resources or a small Active Directory tree without nested groups.

The first flag defines if the WebLogic server will be able to cache some levels of the hierarchy group memberships or not. Some hierarchy functions are as follows:

- **Max Group Hierarchies in Cache**: This defines the size of the cache used to store group membership hierarchies; the default value is 100. Increase this value if you have many nested groups. Oracle recommends a value of 1024.

- **Group Hierarchy Cache TTL**: This defines the number of seconds the cached object will be stored in memory. If you have a quiet static group membership situation, increase this parameter to reduce the queries to the LDAP server and speed up the process exploiting internal cached data. Otherwise, if you have high dynamic membership changes, leave this parameter to the default value of 60 seconds. Oracle recommends setting this value to 10 minutes, but keep in mind all the previous considerations.

Principal Validator Cache

The console path to work with this option is **Security Realms | myrealm | Performance | Enable WebLogic Principal Validator Cache**.

To improve your WebLogic Security Framework performance, keep this option enabled — it's enabled by default. Here, you can set the number of principals to be cached; the default value is 500.

Troubleshooting problems

WebLogic security realm is a fundamental part of the startup phase. Here, in the first instance, the server needs to find the user configured to boot the Admin serve; after this, we need to have all the security providers — including the Authentication Provider — that have a JAAS **Control Flag** set to **OPTIONAL** to complete the initialization phase.

If the initialization phase cannot be completed correctly, the WebLogic server boot fails, displaying an error similar to the following one:

```
<BEA-090870> <The realm "myrealm" failed to be loaded:
```

If you have some problems connecting from the Active Directory side, you can look for some errors in your WebLogic logfiles. Let me show you some error messages, as shown in the following code snippet:

```
Caused by: netscape.ldap.LDAPException: error result (49); 80090308:
LdapErr: DSID-0C0903AA, comment: AcceptSecurityContext error, data
525, v1772; Invalid credentials
```

In the previous error message, the error result (49) error value is encountered when you have provided invalid credentials to log in in the Active Directory Server. In the previous error message, you can also find the LDAP error code 525.

The following are some LDAP error codes and their corresponding descriptions:

- 525: User not found
- 52e: Invalid credentials
- 530: Not permitted to log in at this time
- 531: Not permitted to log in from this workstation
- 532: Password expired
- 533: Account disabled
- 701: Account expired
- 773: User must reset password
- 775: User account locked

The following exception can be encountered when WebLogic can't connect to the Active Directory server. To troubleshoot this problem check your Hostname/IP or Port:

```
Caused by: netscape.ldap.LDAPException: Connection refused (91)
```

If the error (32) error message is raised, then check the filter configurations. This error is encountered when the filter can't find any entries that match the search filter criteria.

To find out more about the LDAP error code, check out the com.novell.ldap. LDAPException class from http://developer.novell.com/documentation/ jldap/jldapenu/api/com/novell/ldap/LDAPException.html, or try to look for the class LDAPException on the Web using your favorite search engine.

User lockout in an Active Directory context

Locking a user is an internal process; it doesn't impact the Active Directory users. If you enable the **User Lockout** option with an Active Directory configuration, remember you need to unlock this user using the WebLogic Admin Console and not using the Active Directory Users and Group Microsoft utility tool.

Think of this as a pre-filter that will cache a user state (enabled or disabled) on the WebLogic layer. It is a better choice for simplifying and centralizing the user security policy lockout on the Active Directory side to disable this feature.

Using Identity Assertion

Typically to support an SSO process, you need to have a `LoginModule` object and an Identity Assertion provider. With these objects, you can exploit tokens stored by the operating system to do the HTTP authorization process without entering username and password and gain access to your secure resources.

The `LoginModule` objects trust that the user has obtained the token by providing the username and password to another authority.

Your token can pass from client to server in different ways such as HTTP headers, cookies, SSL certificates, or other custom mechanisms. The Identity Assertion needs to grab this token and extract the security information to allow access to the secured context paths.

We will be using the SPNEGO Identity Asserter provider in *Chapter 5, Integrating with Kerberos SPNEGO Identity Assertion* to configure the SSO integration in an Active Directory context.

Summary

This chapter covered the basic administration of users and groups of the internal WebLogic LDAP server and some facilities to manage and understand security roles and conditions that you will configure in your server.

This is an important chapter, which covers in detail the parameters and concepts required to attach your WebLogic server in an existing Active Directory environment, tuning and understanding some tricks to improve their performance.

We also discussed the issues that often occur during configuration, along with some typical error codes and their possible solutions.

3
Java EE Security with WebLogic

In this chapter we will see how to implement the standard Java EE security in a WebLogic Enterprise application, with extensive use of real world examples, and finish with a fully complete Maven project that you can deploy with a goal into your development server.

Setting up an Enterprise Maven project

Now we will create, step-by-step, a secure application using Maven, the Oracle Maven plugin, and of course the WebLogic server. A prerequisite for this is that Maven 3 should be installed and properly configured. See the official Maven site for information about how to download and install Maven, at http://maven.apache.org.

Creating the modules with maven-archetype-plugin

The following are the steps we need to follow to create the application that we will be using during this chapter:

1. Create the parent **Project Object Model (POM)** by navigating to the project folder from the command-line tool and launching the following command:

```
mvn archetype:generate -Dversion=1.0-SNAPSHOT
-DgroupId=net.lucamasini.security -DartifactId=chapter3
-DarchetypeArtifactId=pom-root -DarchetypeGroupId=org.codehaus.
mojo.archetypes
```

2. Navigate to the newly created `chapter3` folder using the command-line tool and create the EAR module, as follows:

```
mvn archetype:generate -Dversion=1.0-SNAPSHOT -DgroupId=net.
lucamasini.security -DartifactId=chapter3-ear
-DarchetypeArtifactId=ear-javaee6 -DarchetypeGroupId=org.codehaus.
mojo.archetypes
```

3. In the same way, create an EJB module using the following command:

```
mvn archetype:generate -Dversion=1.0-SNAPSHOT -DgroupId=net.
lucamasini.security -DartifactId=chapter3-ejb
-DarchetypeArtifactId=ejb-javaee6 -DarchetypeGroupId=org.codehaus.
mojo.archetypes
```

4. Finally, create a web module using the following command:

```
mvn archetype:generate -Dversion=1.0-SNAPSHOT -DgroupId=net.
lucamasini.security -DartifactId=chapter3-web
-DarchetypeArtifactId=webapp-javaee6 -DarchetypeGroupId=org.
codehaus.mojo.archetypes
```

To test if everything was correctly configured, we can now launch an install by navigating to the parent folder and executing the following command:

```
mvn install
```

Also check if an EAR file is created in the `chapter3-ear/target` folder; look out for the following file:

`chapter3-ear-1.0-SNAPSHOT.ear`

The EAR file that is created is completely empty, because the Maven EAR plugin looks at the EAR module dependencies to create an enterprise module, so now we need to add the following dependencies into the EAR `pom.xml` file:

```xml
<dependencies>
    <dependency>
        <groupId>${project.groupId}</groupId>
        <artifactId>${parent.artifactId}-ejb</artifactId>
        <version>${project.version}</version>
        <type>ejb</type>
    </dependency>
    <dependency>
        <groupId>${project.groupId}</groupId>
        <artifactId>${parent.artifactId}-web</artifactId>
        <version>${project.version}</version>
        <type>war</type>
    </dependency>
</dependencies>
```

The EAR is not yet a valid Enterprise application for WebLogic; we still need to add an Enterprise Bean into the EJB module. The following is the simplest Bean we can code:

```
package net.lucamasini.security;

import javax.ejb.Stateless;

@Stateless
public class MySimpleNoInterfaceBean {
    public String echo(String input) {
        return "$"+input+"$";
    }
}
```

Finally, we have a working EAR! If you have WebLogic running, you can deploy it and go to the `http://localhost:7001/chapter3-web` URL, after which the following output is displayed:

In case you don't have one, you will learn how to create a domain, launch a server, and deploy the EAR in the upcoming sections.

Installing the WebLogic Server and the WebLogic Maven plugin

A copy of WebLogic Server 12c can be downloaded from Oracle TechNet at `http://www.oracle.com/technetwork/index.html` (the downsized ZIP file for developers should be about 180 MB). After we get the binaries, we need to extract the following two files from the archive by using the following commands for the respective files:

```
unzip /Users/lucamasini/Downloads/wls1211_dev.zip wlserver/server/lib/
wls-maven-plugin.jar.pack
```

```
unzip /Users/lucamasini/Downloads/wls1211_dev.zip wlserver/server/lib/
pom.xml
```

Use the following command to unpack the JAR:

```
unpack200 -r wlserver/server/lib/wls-maven-plugin.jar.pack wlserver/
server/lib/wls-maven-plugin.jar
```

Now that we have everything we need to issue the installation of the plugin into the `localRepository` element, execute the following command:

```
cd wlserver/server/lib
mvn install
mvn install:install-file -Dfile=wls-maven-plugin.jar -DpomFile=pom.xml
```

Also add the plugin `groupId` to the set of the default groups, as follows:

```
<pluginGroups>
  <pluginGroup>com.oracle.weblogic</pluginGroup>
</pluginGroups>
```

Edit the global `settings.xml` file (run `mvn -X | grep global` to see where you can find it in your environment).

Now we must navigate to the EAR folder `chapter3/chapter3-ear` and launch a local installation of WebLogic Server, the one we will use throughout this book, as follows:

```
mvn wls:install -DartifactLocation=/Users/lucamasini/Downloads/wls1211_
dev.zip
```

Now we only need a domain to start, with a username and password for the administrator account, so execute the following command:

```
mvn wls:create-domain -Duser=weblogic -Dpassword=weblog1c
```

64-bit Java Virtual Machine

Under 64-bit systems, we need to enlarge the Permanent Generation space if we are using the HotSpot JVM. Export this environment variable before launching the server, as follows:

```
export USER_MEM_ARGS="-Xms256m -Xmx512m
-XX:CompileThreshold=8000 -XX:PermSize=128m
-XX:MaxPermSize=256m"
```

Finally, we can launch our development server as follows:

```
mvn wls:start-server
```

If everything is right, we can tail the output file (look into the previous command log for stdout) and see if the server is in the RUNNING mode, as follows:

```
<Notice> <WebLogicServer> <BEA-000360> <The server started in RUNNING
mode. >
```

Another test we can do is to check if we can stop it gracefully, using the following:

```
mvn wls:stop-server -Duser=weblogic -Dpassword=weblog1c
```

Configuring wls-maven-plugin into the EAR POM

Since the user and password elements are often used during development, we can configure the plugin on the EAR module's pom.xml file so that we don't need to pass them every time, using the following code snippet:

```
<build>
    <plugins>
        <plugin>
            <groupId>com.oracle.weblogic</groupId>
            <artifactId>wls-maven-plugin</artifactId>
            <version>12.1.1.0</version>
            <configuration>
                <user>weblogic</user>
                <password>weblog1c</password>
                <verbose>true</verbose>
            </configuration>
        </plugin>
    </plugins>
</build>
```

Now that we have configured our development environment, we can start deploying the application into the already running WebLogic Server domain.

Debugging your Enterprise application

Often we need to attach a debugger to our running application; for this we can export the following environment variable before running the start-server goal. This way the Java Virtual Machine will accept connections on the 55822 port from the local/remote debugger.

```
export JAVA_OPTIONS="-Xdebug -Xrunjdwp:transport=dt_so
cket,address=127.0.0.1:55822,suspend=n,server=y"
```

Split deploy and beabuild-maven-plugin

Now that we have our simple application and are running WebLogic Server, we can start developing by simply doing an install using the following command:

```
mvn install
```

This command is executed in the root POM folder. From the EAR module folder, execute the following:

```
wls:deploy -Dname=chapter3-ear
```

There are many reasons why you can't consider this as an agile development lifecycle, but the main reason is that you need to repackage the entire application every time you change a class or a deployment descriptor.

In fact these are two separate problems that are resolved by tools/technologies that are shipped with WebLogic: fast-swap and split deployment, described as follows:

- Split deployment: This is a set of folder layout and WebLogic tools that allow the developer to redeploy the application faster without file copying or application archive creation

- Fast-swap: This is an enhancement to the Java EE runtime class redefinition that allows the reloading of modified classes into a running application's class loader

But you can't use them out of the box in your Maven application, because of the following reasons:

- Fast-swap is not compatible with the 64 bit development box, a common development configuration these days

- Split deployment uses folder layout that is not conventional for Maven users

To solve the fast-swap issue you can use a JVM that supports bytecode reload — like the open source **Dynamic Code Evolution VM (DCEVM)** — or use JRebel from http://zeroturnaround.com/ (which also supports resource reload).

Solving the split deployment problem leads us to write some Maven configurations. We first need to configure the beabuild-generator-plugin into the root pom.xml file as follows:

```
<pluginRepositories>
  <pluginRepository>
      <id>beabuild.release</id>
      <name>Beabuild Release Repository</name>
```

```
        <url>http://maven-beabuild-plugin.googlecode.com/svn/maven2/
releases</url>
    </pluginRepository>
</pluginRepositories>

<build>
    <pluginManagement>
        <plugins>
            <plugin>
                <groupId>org.apache.maven.plugins</groupId>
                <artifactId>beabuild-generator-plugin</artifactId>
                <version>0.9.3</version>
                <executions>
                    <execution>
                    <id>generate</id>
                        <goals>
                            <goal>generate-beabuild</goal>
                        </goals>
                    </execution>
                </executions>
            </plugin>
        </plugins>
    </pluginManagement>
</build>
```

And then into the EAR and WAR modules' `pom.xml` file, insert the following code:

```
<plugin>
    <groupId>org.apache.maven.plugins</groupId>
    <artifactId>beabuild-generator-plugin</artifactId>
</plugin>
```

Now execute `mvn install` from the root POM and a new file will be generated, named `.beabuild.txt`. This will contain a catalog that WebLogic will use in place of the standard Java EE layout to create the application that will be deployed. The plugin knows how Maven works, so you will find in those files all the dependencies required at runtime that are referenced as libraries, classes into target/classes, and the `webapp` folder where our WAR resources are contained.

By working this way we can forget about packaging our application; all we need to do is make an install from the root folder every time we add or remove a dependency, and then run the standard deploy goal pointing as `source` at the folder containing the `.beabuild.txt` file. This can be configured into our EAR module's POM by adding the following tags to the WebLogic plugin configuration:

```
<name>${project.artifactId}</name>
<source>${basedir}/src/main/application</source>
```

We also need the `application.xml` file, which is not mandatory in a Java EE 6 application but is necessary for WebLogic when we use this kind of deployment. The following code, if inserted in the EAR POM, will automatically generate the `application.xml` file for us:

```
<executions>
  <execution>
  <id>generate-application-xml</id>
    <phase>install</phase>
    <goals>
      <goal>generate-application-xml</goal>
      <goal>ear</goal>
   </goals>
  </execution>
</executions>
```

We also need to exclude the `.beabuild.txt` file. From the generated EAR or WebLogic will try to do split deployment in production mode when this file is found and tell where `application.xml` will be generated, by using the following code:

```
<generatedDescriptorLocation>${project.basedir}/src/main/application/
META-INF/</generatedDescriptorLocation>
<earSourceExcludes>.beabuild.txt</earSourceExcludes>
```

The previous tag in the EAR plugin configuration does all the dirty work. Now we can run `install` from the root module for the first time so that `application.xml` and `.beabuild.txt` will be generated, by using the following command:

mvn install

From now on, deploy our application from the EAR module with only the following simple command:

mvn wls:deploy

We don't need to package the application anymore!

To summarize, using a JVM that reloads classes and resources and the beabuild-plugin, our development lifecycle will be able to do the following:

- Compile with the IDE for changes to the source code
- If you also change some deployment descriptors or annotations, then launch `mvn wls:deploy` from the EAR module, without packaging the application

That's what we call an agile development workflow!

Launching our Hello Maven and WebLogic world application

Now that we have a running WebLogic Server and an application configured for an agile development, we can simply launch our application as follows:

```
mvn wls:deploy
```

Now we can call `http://localhost:7001/chapter3-web` to see the starter application in action.

Securing the web module

The first resource we want to protect is the web resource, a servlet, as follows:

```
package net.lucamasini.security;

@WebServlet(name="MyWorkServlet",
        urlPatterns={"/myprotectedresource"})
public class MyProtectedServlet extends HttpServlet {
    @Override
    protected void doGet(HttpServletRequest req,
                    HttpServletResponse resp)
        throws ServletException, IOException {
        Principal userPrincipal = req.getUserPrincipal();
resp.getWriter().println(userPrincipal!=null?userPrincipal.getName():
"anonymous");
    }
}
```

Here we can see the power of Java EE 6: we don't need to write XML to declare a servlet and to bind it to a URL, a single annotation is enough. Now, after compiling and launching, the deploy goal will allow us to call `http://localhost:7001/chapter3-web/myprotectedresource` and see the string `anonymous`; this means our servlet has been deployed and the user is still anonymous.

Now we can go a step further and protect the web resource. Again, a simple annotation does the work without the need to edit `web.xml`, as follows:

```
@ServletSecurity(@HttpConstraint(rolesAllowed={"my-user"}))
```

If we call the URL now, entering WebLogic's administrator principals (`weblogic/weblogic` when we created the domain with the `create-domain` goal) should obtain a **403 FORBIDDEN** HTTP status code. This means that the user has been recognized, but has no rights to access the resource. This may sound a little strange: the Administrator group can do everything in our domain but it is perfectly valid that our application doesn't trust such users!

The problem is that we never specified to WebLogic that the `my-user` role is mapped to the Administrator's principal.

Now we have to decide what kind of role-mapping strategy we need to use. A typical Java EE mapping is done using custom deployment descriptors (like the `weblogic.xml` custom deployment descriptor), but this has the prerequisite of knowing about the groups and users that will use our application.

If, instead, we can't know in advance which are users and which are groups, we need to change those mappings without redeployment, or if the mapping is too complex to be defined using a one-to-many relationship (a role mapped to many principals), we have another chance in WebLogic using its runtime custom Roles Mapper.

Standard DD mapping

Let's start with the standard DD mapping. For this, finally, we need to write XML, the custom deployment descriptor `weblogic.xml`, into the `src/main/webapp/WEB-INF` folder, as follows:

```xml
<?xml version="1.0" encoding="UTF-8"?>
<weblogic-web-app xmlns="http://xmlns.oracle.com/weblogic/weblogic-web-app">
    <security-role-assignment>
        <role-name>my-user</role-name>
        <principal-name>users</principal-name>
    </security-role-assignment>
</weblogic-web-app>
```

Here, we are using one of the embedded groups in WebLogic; all users are implicitly also members of the `users` group, and this time calling the URL will work and we will see **weblogic** appear on our browser.

Custom Roles Mapping

Mapping of roles is done by WebLogic Server XACML Role Mapping Provider, which allows us to use the console or its runtime MBean, to declare roles under certain conditions. In fact, we can do everything that the standard DD does, such as declare a role if one or more groups are principals of the current subject, but also declare rules like is in development mode or in not into the group. For a complete list you can view the official documentation.

Now we start doing the same stuff done into the DD, that is, declaring that every principal that is in the `users` group has the role `my-user`. We could do this in a very fast and intuitive way using the Web Console, but in this chapter we will do everything using Maven and this is not an exception.

We must create the file `create-roles.py` under the `chapter3-ear` folder with the following content:

```
connect('weblogic','weblog1c')
xacml = cmo.getSecurityConfiguration().getDefaultRealm().lookupRoleMap
per('XACMLRoleMapper')
xacml.createRole(None,'my-user',None)
xacml.setRoleExpression(None,'my-user', 'Grp(users)')
```

And then run the following WLST script with the Maven plugin:

```
mvn wls:wlst -DfileName=create-roles.py
```

By doing this, we create a global role called `my-user` that we can check under the console at **Home | Summary of Security Realms | myrealm | Realm Roles | Global Roles**.

> **Deployment roles**
> We are not limited to creating global roles; we can also create a role that is local to a specific deployed application

Of course, calling `http://localhost:7001/chapter3-web/myprotectedresource` will have the same desired effect of showing us the current logged in user.

Programmatic security

There are certain situations when we can't rely only on declarative security; when we need another level of intelligence to understand if the user can or cannot access the requested resource. In effect, the semantics of the standard declarative security is quite primitive—a list of principals in logical OR; not enough for many business case.

Imagine, for instance, that you need to check if a user is a member of at least two groups, if the time of the day is in a certain range, or if the user is contained in a business table.

In all these cases, we need to code the security of our application, and Java EE doesn't help much. On the web tier, we have only a single API call that can tell us if a user has or does not have a certain role. We can add the following line of code to our servlet to experiment:

```
resp.getWriter().
        println("my-user: "+req.isUserInRole("my-user"));
```

Now, calling our URL will also display **my-user: true**, because we are also using declarative security to allow access to that resource. Usually, we must disable declarative security when we need programmatic security and then code our business rule.

Programmatic security with WebLogic XACML provider

Under WebLogic, we have the chance to skip security coding when using Customer Roles. In fact, when we declare our roles we have a richer semantic, and if you need a user that is a member of two groups—users and Administrators—you can write the following:

```
Grp(users)&Grp(Administrators)
```

But this Provider is not limited to this. We can also do the following:

- Negate conditions
- Check if the server is in the development mode
- Check if date and time follow some conditions, such as day-of-the-week and range-of-hours
- Contextual elements, like the current HTTP request or the socket port

Using the XACML Role Mapping Provider in a correct way can spare us from coding programmatic security using a well-defined standard like OASIS's **eXtensible Access Control Markup Language (XACML)**.

A RESTful and secure EJB component

Java EE 6 not only allows us to package EJBs into their own module, but also to deploy our Beans directly into the WAR module that will use them. We will see how to secure both of these scenarios.

Bean packaged into the WAR module

Often, we don't need to package Enterprise Beans into a separated module; we can collocate them inside the same WAR client module and simplify our application architecture. Now, we will develop a simple EJB that will be injected into the existing MyProtectedServlet class. We will also see the security context to be passed and the configuration we need to do.

Let's start simple; we can code this really simple Stateless Bean with no interface view, as shown in the following code snippet:

```
package net.lucamasini.security;

import javax.ejb.Stateless;

@Stateless
public class NoInterfaceBeanInWarModule {
    public String echo(String input) {
        return "$"+input+"$";
    }
}
```

This Java file must be in the same folder containing our servlet, and we also need to modify the servlet itself to include the injection. Use the following code:

```
@EJB
private NoInterfaceBeanInWarModule service;
```

And add the service invocation as follows:

```
resp.getWriter().println("echo:"+service.echo("echo"));
```

Nothing special until now, we can find many tutorials that show us how to do this. If we call the usual URL now, we will see another line into the browser that displays the following:

echo:$echo$

When do we often change metadata?

In this section, we will often change the annotation for our experiment, so my advice is to launch the deploy goal every time to prevent incurring unexpected results. This will be unnecessary during the standard development lifecycle.

So let's start introducing security into our EJB by adding the following annotation to the Bean class:

```
@RolesAllowed("my-user")
```

Now, by calling the URL again we will see the same output, but the Bean is now secured. In fact, every call to any method will check if the principal has the `my-user` role, and if not a security error will be raised. Let's check this by adding the same annotation to the single method with another role, as follows:

```
@RolesAllowed("my-special-user")
```

Now we are not allowed to access the test URL; we will see the following error message on the server log (and also on the browser window):

```
javax.ejb.EJBAccessException: [EJB:010160] Security violation:
User weblogic has insufficient permission to access EJB
type=<ejb>, application=chapter3-ear, module=/chapter3-web,
ejb=NoInterfaceBeanInWarModule, method=echo, methodInterface=Local,
signature={java.lang.String}.
```

The exception is very clear and tells us that the currently logged-in `user` is `weblogic`, and also displays the signature of the method that we are trying to call, to let us quickly identify the problem. To solve it, we can add role mapping to the custom deployment descriptor or use the XACML Role Mapper. In the latter case, we can add the following two lines to the `create-roles.py` Python file used for our servlet:

```
xacmlRoleMapper.createRole(None, 'my-special-user',None)
xacmlRoleMapper.setRoleExpression(None, 'my-special-user',
'Grp(users)')
```

And then launch the WLST to execute it as follows:

```
mvn wls:wlst -DfileName=create-roles.py
```

This fixes the problem and allows us to execute our servlet again. But, we want to go a step further and configure this using a different group and WebLogic's custom deployment descriptor.

The first step is to configure the internal LDAP server, creating a new `bookreaders` group and then adding a new user, `luca`, to that group. This can be done with the Admin Console as we have seen in *Chapter 2, WebLogic Security Realm*. Then we must create the `weblogic-ejb-jar.xml` file in the `WEB-INF` folder with the following content:

```xml
<?xml version="1.0" encoding="UTF-8"?>
<weblogic-ejb-jar xmlns="http://xmlns.oracle.com/weblogic/weblogic-
ejb-jar">
    <security-role-assignment>
        <role-name>my-special-user</role-name>
        <principal-name>bookreaders</principal-name>
    </security-role-assignment>
</weblogic-ejb-jar>
```

By redeploying our example, we can now successfully call our test URL using the new configured user, `luca`.

Changing Security Identity with RunAs

There are some use cases where we need to call some business methods without having the right to do so. For instance, you may need to call a method that is usually called by administrative users from a non-administrative account.

The solution for that use case is the `RunAs` annotation, which allows us to impersonate any principal, because by default Java EE trusts identities between containers and we don't need any special configuration for this to work.

We can see this at work in our application by removing the newly created user/group and any role mapping, and then adding the following annotation in the Bean class definition:

```java
@RunAs("my-special-user")
```

Of course, we then need to specify the real user that will run with that role, inside the `weblogic-ejb-jar.xml` custom DD, as follows:

```xml
<run-as-role-assignment>
    <role-name>my-special-user</role-name>
    <run-as-principal-name>weblogic</run-as-principal-name>
</run-as-role-assignment>
```

This enables the trust between containers; the EJB container will now trust that weblogic—authenticated on the serlvet container—has the my-special-user role and as such can also invoke its methods.

Securing the EJB module

We have just finished exploring how we can secure servlets and EJBs in the WAR module. The coding and configuration required is not different if we decide to deploy a Bean into an EJB Module; the only difference is that the weblogic-ejb-jar.xml file must be written into the src/main/resources/META-INF folder, and that the WAR and EJB Modules inside an EAR have different class loaders.

Of course, if your EAR has many WARs that share business logic, this is the desired deployment configuration; but if your application is composed of a single WAR and a single EJB, consider switching to a WAR-only deployment.

Summary

In this chapter, we learned how to set up WebLogic for development, how to develop a simple Enterprise application, and how we can configure security specific to WebLogic.

Creating Custom
Authentication Providers
with Maven

In this chapter we will learn how to implement a custom provider that integrates some of our legacy SSO systems.

Developing a provider consists of the following tasks:

- Creating and configuring a Maven project
- Writing our MBean delegate
- Developing a JAAS `LoginModule` that interacts with our SSO and returns Principals to WebLogic

As we shall see, the hardest work will be configuring Maven to have a reproducible and industry-ready project that can create the MBean JAR file for us.

The Maven project

There is no WebLogic MBeanMaker plugin in our application and also the existing tool is not really Maven friendly.

WebLogic MBeanMaker

This is a command-line utility that generates all the files you need to form an **MBean type**, from partial Java classes to contract interfaces and some custom files used by WebLogic itself to introspect the MBean once it is deployed in JAR inside the system class loader.

What we will do is an integration of the existing technologies into Maven using the `maven-antrun-plugin` plugin as a bridge between these two worlds. These technologies are so invasive that we will have to disable some standard and common Maven plugins such as `maven-jar-plugin` and `maven-install-plugin`. In a sense, the work of the compile plugin will be done by this piece of ancient BEA technology.

But all of this makes sense if we want to have a piece of software that can be integrated into modern build systems, and if we want to have a good development environment where we can work in a write-deploy-run lifecycle.

Creating the Maven project

We will start simple, with the shortest and simplest Maven POM we can have, as shown in the following code snippet:

```xml
<?xml version="1.0" encoding="UTF-8"?>
<project xmlns="http://maven.apache.org/POM/4.0.0"
         xmlns:xsi="http://www.w3.org/2001/XMLSchema-instance"
         xsi:schemaLocation="http://maven.apache.org/POM/4.0.0 http://
maven.apache.org/xsd/maven-4.0.0.xsd">
    <modelVersion>4.0.0</modelVersion>

    <groupId>net.lucamasini.security</groupId>
    <artifactId>chapter-4-auth-provider</artifactId>
    <version>1.0-SNAPSHOT</version>

</project>
```

Here, we didn't specify a parent POM and we left the standard JAR packaging as it is—even if this is not managed by Maven—because it will be done directly by WebLogic MBeanMaker. We are not going to specify, here, all the properties that are needed because there are too many and they will be introduced progressively as we proceed with this chapter.

Dependencies

Our projects need some dependencies from the WebLogic binaries to compile.
The different binaries that need to be added are explained in the following steps:

1. First we need to add the JAR containing the custom WebLogic Security API
    of our MBean, as shown in the following code snippet:

```
<dependency>
    <groupId>com.bea.core</groupId>
    <artifactId>commons.security.api</artifactId>
    <version>1.1.0.0_6-2-0-0</version>
    <scope>system</scope>
    <systemPath>
     ${middleware.home}/modules/
     com.bea.core.common.security.api_1.1.0.0_6-2-0-0.jar
    </systemPath>
</dependency>
```

2. Then, we need to add a JAR containing classes that we will use in
    our `LoginModule` (`WLSUser` and `WLSGroup`), as shown in the following
    code snippet:

```
<dependency>
    <groupId>com.bea.core</groupId>
    <artifactId>weblogic.security</artifactId>
    <version>1.1.0.0_6-2-0-0</version>
    <scope>system</scope>
    <systemPath>
     ${middleware.home}/modules/
     com.bea.core.weblogic.security_1.1.0.0_6-2-0-0.jar
    </systemPath>
</dependency>
```

3. Finally we need the WebLogic mega JAR where most of the used classes
    are located; it can be added using the following code:

```
<dependency>
    <groupId>oracle</groupId>
    <artifactId>weblogic</artifactId>
    <version>${weblogic.version}</version>
    <scope>system</scope>
    <systemPath>
     ${middleware.home}/wlserver/server/lib/weblogic.jar
    </systemPath>
</dependency>
```

4. As can be seen from this first piece of POM, we need to add two properties; one of them points to WebLogic installation, as shown in the following code:

```
<middleware.home>/path/to/wls1211_dev</middleware.home>
```

5. The other is the version we are developing on, as shown in the following code:

```
<weblogic.version>12.1.1.0</weblogic.version>
```

Reconfiguring standard plugins

Another easy step is to reconfigure some common Maven plugins, such as compile and resources. Inside the `<build>` tag, we add the following code:

```
<plugins>
    <plugin>
        <artifactId>maven-compiler-plugin</artifactId>
        <version>2.0.2</version>
        <configuration>
            <encoding>UTF-8</encoding>
            <source>${maven.compiler.source}</source>
            <target>${maven.compiler.target}</target>
        </configuration>
    </plugin>
    <plugin>
        <artifactId>maven-resources-plugin</artifactId>
        <version>2.5</version>
        <configuration>
            <encoding>UTF-8</encoding>
        </configuration>
        <executions>
            <execution>
                <id>default-install</id>
                <phase>install</phase>
                <goals>
                    <goal>copy-resources</goal>
                </goals>
                <configuration>
                    <outputDirectory>
                    ${domain.dir}/lib/mbeantypes
                </outputDirectory>
                    <resources>
                        <resource>
                            <directory>
```

```
                    ${project.build.directory}
                </directory>
                        <includes>
                            <include>
                    ${project.build.finalName}.jar
                    </include>
                        </includes>
                    </resource>
                </resources>
            </configuration>
        </execution>
    </executions>
  </plugin>
</plugins>
```

Here, we configure UTF-8 as standard encoding so that it is platform independent (remember to configure your source editor) and we set source/target version for the javac compiler. Of course, we need to define the following two new properties:

```
<maven.compiler.source>1.6</maven.compiler.source>
<maven.compiler.target>1.6</maven.compiler.target>
```

As already explained, the WebLogic MBeanMaker takes care of packaging the created artifact, so we need to disable the standard maven-jar-plugin plugin. Moreover, the out-of-the-box install goal does not make any sense in this environment, so we configure an ad hoc execution of maven-resources-plugin that moves the generated JAR file inside the correct folder, because of which we can also disable the standard maven-install-plugin plugin, as shown in the following code snippet:

```
<plugin>
    <artifactId>maven-jar-plugin</artifactId>
    <version>2.4</version>
    <executions>
        <execution>
            <id>default-jar</id>
            <phase>none</phase>
        </execution>
    </executions>
</plugin>
<plugin>
    <artifactId>maven-install-plugin</artifactId>
    <version>2.3.1</version>
    <executions>
        <execution>
            <id>default-install</id>
```

```
                <phase>none</phase>
            </execution>
        </executions>
    </plugin>
```

We can see that in order to disable one of the standard Maven plugins, all we need to do is bind its internal execution ID to the none execution phase.

The install plugin is replaced by the default-install execution of maven-resources-plugin, where we tell it to move the generated JAR inside the WebLogic domain's lib/mbeantype folder, which is the default folder for custom Providers. For that we need to define a new property, as shown in the following code snippet:

```
<domain.dir>/path/to/your/domain</domain.dir>
```

The path should point to the folder where we created the development domain.

Now another plugin, this time a custom plugin from Codehaus' Mojo project, one that does something that Maven should do on its own—add another source folder.

Quite often you have more than one place where sources are placed because one of them was written by a developer and the others are autogenerated. This kind of configuration is not possible using the standard set of Maven plugins. Luckily, this simple plugin that does a lot of other interesting things, allows us to add other folders as source folders. This plugin is used in the following code snippet:

```
<plugin>
    <groupId>org.codehaus.mojo</groupId>
    <artifactId>build-helper-maven-plugin</artifactId>
    <version>1.5</version>
    <executions>
        <execution>
            <id>add-source</id>
            <phase>generate-sources</phase>
            <goals>
                <goal>add-source</goal>
            </goals>
            <configuration>
                <sources>
                    <source>${generated.sources.dir}</source>
                </sources>
            </configuration>
        </execution>
    </executions>
</plugin>
```

The execution of the `add-source` goal is bound to the `generate-sources` phase so that everything is consistent within this POM configuration. What is `${generated.sources.dir}`? It is a new property, defined as follows:

```
<generated.sources.dir>
  ${project.build.directory}/generated-source
</generated.sources.dir>
```

It is the destination where we will tell WebLogic MBeanMaker to write its custom generated classes.

The last simple task we will do inside this POM is to enable resource filtering. Again inside the `<build>` tag, we add the following code:

```
<resources>
   <resource>
      <filtering>true</filtering>
      <directory>src/main/resources</directory>
   </resource>
</resources>
```

Adding WebLogic MBeanMaker to the POM

WebLogic's MBean is an old BEA-patented technology and is based on the following:

- An XML MBean definition file
- A set of APIs
- A generator that—in two steps—generates the MBean that executes our `LoginModule` and then packages it for deployment under WebLogic as an Authentication Provider.

That said, it is a really old piece of software and it's tied to WebLogic and its custom development environment, based on Ant and proprietary APIs. Integration with Maven is possible in the following two ways:

- The main road: Writing a custom plugin that uses Oracle's utility and also configures the execution phase
- Let it think: Deceive MBeanMaker to think it is running inside Ant using the `mave-antrun-plugin` plugin

Of course, the former is a better solution that can spare us a lot of time configuring the POM, but you need to have some time to write and maintain it over an extended period of time and over different WebLogic versions.

Using the latter solution instead is far less elegant because we need to write some old Ant XML configuration. But this way it's really easy to integrate it with Maven.

That said, we will explore the second solution and we will configure Ant to execute the generator for us. The first thing to do is to configure the plugin and its dependencies, as shown in the following code snippet:

```
<plugin>
    <artifactId>maven-antrun-plugin</artifactId>
    <version>1.3</version>
    <dependencies>
        <dependency>
            <groupId>weblogic</groupId>
            <artifactId>weblogic</artifactId>
            <version>${weblogic.version}</version>
            <scope>system</scope>
            <systemPath>
        ${middleware.home}/wlserver/server/lib/weblogic.jar
            </systemPath>
        </dependency>
    </dependencies>
    <executions>
    ...
    ...
```

Then, we will code the two `execution` tags. First, the MBean definition file is read and then the intermediary files are created, as shown in the following code snippet:

```
<execution>
    <id>generate-mbean</id>
    <phase>process-resources</phase>
    <goals>
        <goal>run</goal>
    </goals>
    <configuration>
        <tasks>
            <java fork="true" classname="weblogic.management.commo.
WebLogicMBeanMaker" classpathref="maven.plugin.classpath">
                <jvmarg
            value="-DMDF=${project.build.outputDirectory}/
                PacktSiteUsersAuthentication.xml" />
                <jvmarg
            value="-Dfiles=${project.build.outputDirectory}" />
                <jvmarg value="-DcreateStubs=true" />
                <jvmarg value="-Dverbose=true" />
```

```
            </java>
        </tasks>
    </configuration>
</execution>
```

Here, we launch the WebLogic MBeanMaker telling it to parse the XML file inside the output folder. This works because we linked this execution to the `process-resources` and so we can be sure that `maven-resources-plugin` has filtered our resources and placed them inside the configured output folder. We also tell it to place the intermediate files inside the output folder and to eventually overwrite existing stubs (not in our case because we are using a generated folder). Finally, we enable the verbose mode to display any important information in case we need them.

In the second `execution`, the intermediary files and developer code is compiled and packaged as an MBean, as shown in the following code snippet:

```
<execution>
    <id>generate-jar</id>
    <phase>compile</phase>
    <goals>
        <goal>run</goal>
    </goals>
    <configuration>
        <tasks>
            <java fork="true"
  classname="weblogic.management.commo.WebLogicMBeanMaker"
  classpathref="maven.plugin.classpath">
                <jvmarg value="-DMJF=${jar.file}" />
                <jvmarg value="-Dfiles=${project.build.
outputDirectory}" />
                <jvmarg value="-DcreateStubs=true" />
                <jvmarg value="-DpreserveStubs=true" />
                <jvmarg value="-Dverbose=true" />
                <arg value="-preserveStubs" />
            </java>
            <move
            todir="${generated.sources.dir}/${package.dir}"
            file="${project.build.outputDirectory}/
                PacktSiteUsersAuthenticationImpl.java" />
            <move todir="${generated.sources.dir}">
                <fileset
              dir="${project.build.outputDirectory}">
                    <include name="**/*.java" />
                </fileset>
            </move>
```

```
        </tasks>
      </configuration>
    </execution>
```

Of course, here we need to define two new Maven properties; the first points to the JAR file that we want to be generated, as shown in the following code snippet:

```
<jar.file>
${project.build.directory}/${project.build.finalName}.jar
</jar.file>
```

The second is used to preserve package structure during the move task, as shown in the following code:

```
<package.dir>
net/lucamasini/security
</package.dir>
```

Maven configuration is now completed. This POM can be used as a template for every Authentication Provider we need to do, and we can proceed to the core implementation of the MBean, starting with its XML definition.

Defining the MBean with an MDF File

The central point of our development iteration is the MDF file, where we define the MBean that is a wrapper of `LoginModule`, which we will implement. This is a custom XML and you need the `commo.dtd` file that can be found inside the WebLogic installation (under the `$MW_HOME/wl_server/server/lib` folder) and copy it inside the `src/main/resources` folder of your project, because from now on it will be referenced using the `SYSTEM` document type, as shown in the following code snippet:

```
<?xml version="1.0" ?>
<!DOCTYPE MBeanType SYSTEM "commo.dtd">
```

Of course, the main tag is named `MBeanType` and defines how the MBean class will be generated; the `MBeanType` is defined as follows:

```
<MBeanType
Name = "PacktSiteUsersAuthentication"
DisplayName = "PacktSiteUsersAuthentication"
Package = "net.lucamasini.security"
Extends =
"weblogic.management.security.authentication.Authenticator"
PersistPolicy = "OnUpdate"
>
```

Every attribute of this tag is very important, starting with the name that will be used to define a new XML schema type for the security namespace inside the WebLogic's `config.xml` file, as defined in the following code snippet:

```
<sec:authentication-provider
xmlns:ext="http://xmlns.oracle.com/weblogic/security/extension"
xsi:type="ext:packt-site-users-authenticationType">
  <sec:name>packt</sec:name>
  <sec:control-flag>OPTIONAL</sec:control-flag>
</sec:authentication-provider>
```

Here, we can see that `xsi:type` is the MBean name lowered, with a - between lowercase letters and with `Type` as a suffix.

The `DisplayName` attribute is instead used inside the WebLogic console and that is what we see in the drop-down menu when we add a new Authentication Provider.

`Package` is the Java package of the generated artifacts and `Extends` is the standard MBean we decided to extend — `weblogic.management.security.authentication.Authenticator` — when we develop an Authentication Provider.

The last attribute — `PersistPolicy = "OnUpdate"` — tells to generate an MBean that will write itself in the storage file (usually the `config.xml`) every time one of its attributes is modified.

Finally, we can run an `mvn` install to generate our Authentication Provider, as shown in the following command:

mvn install

This provider is not yet a working provider, but we can catch a glimpse of what we are going to build.

It can be installed under the WebLogic console, but then WebLogic will refuse to start with a **[Security:097533]SecurityProvider service class name for PackProvider is not specified** error message because we haven't yet configured the MDF, and nor have we written the implementation of our MBean. But apart from this, WebLogic knows what we have just generated and tries to use it (if you are panicking about your WebLogic domain, just delete the `sec:` section inside the `config.xml` file).

Peering inside the target folder, we can notice a special class under the `weblogic.management.security` package; in our sample it will be named `CHAPTER4_AUTH_PROVIDER_1_0_SNAPSHOT1345106773809855000BeanInfoFactory`. It is named with the name of the MBean JAR file along with the current time in milliseconds, which is different every time we do the install (for that always remember to do a clean before install). This class is a factory that, given the interface, references the standard JavaBean's `BeanInfo` class of our MBean implementation.

We can proceed with writing our MDF and adding the configuration for `ProviderClassName` as follows:

```
<MBeanAttribute
Name = "ProviderClassName"
Type = "java.lang.String"
Writeable = "false"
Default = "&quot;net.lucamasini.security.PacktAuthProviderImpl&quot;"
/>
```

Please note that we need to use the `&quot;` XML entity because the `ProviderClassName` attribute needs a value between quotes, but these are now used by the XML file itself.

If not, when we relaunch the install and start WebLogic, we will get a completely different error message—**[Security:097534]Failed to obtain an instance of class net. lucamasini.security.PacktAuthProviderImpl**. This is because we've now specified which class will be our MBean implementation and WebLogic tries to create a new instance of a class that doesn't exist yet.

The next two attributes that we are going to add are those that the WebLogic administrator will see when he/she will configures the provider; these attributes are as follows:

```
<MBeanAttribute
Name = "Description"
Type = "java.lang.String"
Writeable = "false"
Default = "&quot;WebLogic Packt Authentication Provider&quot;"
/>

<MBeanAttribute
Name = "Version"
Type = "java.lang.String"
Writeable = "false"
Default = "&quot;1.0&quot;"
/>
```

In `description` and `version`, we can add whatever we prefer; these are two informative strings and we can check this in the `MBeanImplBeanInfo` class by looking for these two properties.

Finally, we add a real configuration property, the URL that will be used by our provider to interact with our legacy SSO system, as shown in the following code:

```
<MBeanAttribute
Name = "URL"
Type = "java.lang.String"
Writeable = "true"
Default = "&quot;${authentication.services.url}&quot;"
/>
```

In a different manner from the other attributes, this can also be written using the console (or directly into the `config.xml` file) by our system administrator. We are not hardcoding the URL inside the MDF file, but using Maven's resource filtering so that we can configure this parameter inside our POM—maybe with different values between our environments (development, stage, and production).

Of course, our POM must be enriched with the following new property:

```
<authentication.services.url>
    http://localhost:8080/sso.jsp
</authentication.services.url>
```

Our MDF file configuration is completed. We can now code the MBean's delegate implementation class.

Writing the MBean implementation

Every Authentication Provider must implement the `weblogic.security.spi.AuthenticationProviderV2` interface, which is the real contract between WebLogic's Security Services and our implementation, as shown in the following code snippet:

```
public class PacktAuthProviderImpl implements AuthenticationProviderV2

{
    private static final Logger LOGGER = Logger.
getLogger(PacktAuthProviderImpl.class.getSimpleName());

    @Override
    public void initialize(ProviderMBean mbean, SecurityServices
services) {
```

```
        LOGGER.info("PacktAuthProviderImpl.initialize");
    }

    @Override
    public String getDescription() {
        return null;
    }

    @Override
    public void shutdown() {
        LOGGER.info("PacktAuthProviderImpl.shutdown");
    }

    @Override
    public AppConfigurationEntry getLoginModuleConfiguration() {
        return null;
    }

    @Override
    public AppConfigurationEntry getAssertionModuleConfiguration() {
        return null;
    }

    @Override
    public PrincipalValidator getPrincipalValidator() {
        return null;
    }

    @Override
    public IdentityAsserterV2 getIdentityAsserter() {
        return null;
    }
}
```

And yes, now you can install and configure the provider in your domain; you will see the following single line of log:

```
net.lucamasini.security.PacktAuthProviderImpl initialize
INFO: PacktAuthProviderImpl.initialize
```

It's not much, but it means that our configuration and infrastructure is working fine. From now on, finally, we will really code there, giving behavior to the PacktAuthProviderImpl class that WebLogic now knows is a custom provider.

Initializing the provider

Every framework has its own lifecycle, and every lifecycle has a start and an end. For `AuthenticationProviderV2` these are the callback methods `initialize` and `shutdown`, where we can not only eventually instantiate our custom objects but also grab configuration from the MBean that wraps our class and communicates with the console. In this simple implementation, we don't need to do anything inside `shutdown`, so we'll leave the current one that logs a line when it is called.

Instead, a lot must be done inside the `initialize` method, where we receive the MBean instance and the Security Service, which is our actual container. The first thing we need to do is cast the generic `ProviderMBean` to our custom MBean so that we can use our specific attributes, as follows:

```
PacktSiteUsersAuthenticationMBean myMBean =
(PacktSiteUsersAuthenticationMBean) mbean;
```

Now that we have our specific instance, we can save the configuration for later use using the following code snippet:

```
description = myMBean.getDescription() + "\n" + myMBean.getVersion();
url = myMBean.getURL();
```

Here `description` and `url` are two instance string fields. We also need to save an instance of `AppConfigurationEntry.LoginModuleControlFlag`, which is a JAAS version of an enum type (old style Java) that tells us if our Security Provider is mandatory or not. This can be done as follows:

```
String flag = myMBean.getControlFlag();
try {
controlFlag =(AppConfigurationEntry.LoginModuleControlFlag)
AppConfigurationEntry.LoginModuleControlFlag.class.getField(flag).
get(null);
} catch (Exception e) {
    throw new IllegalArgumentException("invalid flag value" + flag,e);
}
```

In this first stage, we can print the configuration output on WebLogic's Server log so that we can be sure that we call the correct parameter and our simple parsing code is working fine. Use the following code:

```
LOGGER.info("ControlFlag: "+controlFlag);
LOGGER.info("Description: "+description);
LOGGER.info("URL: "+url);
```

We should see something like the following:

```
INFO: ControlFlag: LoginModuleControlFlag: optional
INFO: Description: WebLogic Packt Authentication Provider
1.0
INFO: URL: http://external-user.intra.net/checkUserLogin
```

Implementation of the provider

Our implementation is almost finished; we now need to implement the remaining method, getDescription. This is quite straightforward, as shown in the following code:

```
@Override
public String getDescription() {
  return description;
}
```

While getIdentityAsserter will continue to return null (as we are coding an Authentication Provider), we still need to implement the Principal Validator, and for that we can use a built-in validator that comes with WebLogic, as shown in the following code snippet:

```
@Override
public PrincipalValidator getPrincipalValidator() {
  return new
    weblogic.security.provider.PrincipalValidatorImpl();
}
```

Finally, the configuration of JAAS LoginModule, which will actually do the authentication. We will not use any standard LoginModule, rather we will use our own:

```
@Override
public AppConfigurationEntry getLoginModuleConfiguration() {
  return new AppConfigurationEntry(
    "net.lucamasini.security.PacktLoginModuleImpl",
   controlFlag,
    new HashMap<String, Object>() {{
    put("url", url);
    }}
  );
}

@Override
public AppConfigurationEntry getAssertionModuleConfiguration() {
```

```
    return getLoginModuleConfiguration();
}
```

We can now install and start WebLogic. Strangely, it will not complain about the fact that the `PacktLoginModuleImpl` class is missing; it will merely ignore this Authentication Provider during the login process. This can be seen as an error, but it is a good and conservative practice and in case we want/need to check if our configuration has been read correctly, we can always enable the **atn** debug flag by going to **weblogic.security.atn** in the console or start up script and look for `PacktLoginModuleImpl`.

Custom JAAS LoginModule

Fortunately, `LoginModule` uses a standard JAAS API and as such is well documented in many books and on the Internet. Here, we will write the simplest `LoginModule` that solves our problem of validating the principals over a legacy external SSO system using the HTTP protocol. As a didactical support, we will also write in the log when the Security Services container will call our method so that we can figure out when and how many times they are called.

Keep in mind that `LoginModule` is a stateful Bean; it must retain configuration data when it is initialized, and from the login callback state to the commit state (or abort or whatever) it must keep the state to answer in a correct and expected way.

Let's start with the definition; the instance fields will be declared as and when we need them. The code for our custom `LoginModule` is as follows:

```
public class PacktLoginModuleImpl implements LoginModule {
   private final static Logger LOGGER = Logger.
     getLogger(PacktLoginModuleImpl.class.getSimpleName());

   private Subject subject;
   private CallbackHandler callbackHandler;
  private String url;

   public void
   initialize( Subject subject, CallbackHandler callbackHandler, Map
sharedState, Map options )
{
      LOGGER.info("PacktLoginModuleImpl.initialize");

      this.subject = subject;
      this.callbackHandler = callbackHandler;
      this.url = options.get("url").toString();
   }
```

Here we simply print the log information saying that a new instance of LoginModule has been created, and save the information needed for the authentication process, explained as follows:

- subject: This is the current subject that we will enrich with our principals in case of a successful login
- callbackhandler: This is our official supplier of credentials to authenticate the user (in this example, we will use the canonical couple — the username and password combination)
- url: This is our very own configuration, the legacy SSO system URL

The login() method

After we have correctly initialized the object, we can expect the container to call the login() method to give us a chance of authentication. Use the following code:

```
public boolean login() throws LoginException {
  LOGGER.fine("PacktLoginModuleImpl.login");
```

Like we said, we decided to log all our method calls in this LoginModule, but the first real thing that we need to do is to define which Callback methods will give us the correct information to accept or decline user identity, as shown in the following code snippet:

```
Callback[] callbacks = new Callback[]{
        new NameCallback("username: "),
        new PasswordCallback("password: ", false)
};

try {
    callbackHandler.handle(callbacks);
} catch (Exception e) {
    LOGGER.throwing("PacktLoginModuleImpl", "login", e);
    throw new LoginException(e.getMessage());
}
```

Here we define two Callback methods, one that will ask the system for a username and another for the password, and then we use the callbackHandler interface that we saved during the initialization state to populate them, so that we can then extract what we need, as shown in the following code:

```
PasswordCallback passwordCallback = (PasswordCallback)
callbacks[1];
    char[] passwordChars = passwordCallback.getPassword();
    passwordCallback.clearPassword();
    final String password = new String(passwordChars);
```

Here, we clear the `PasswordCallback` internal state after we get the password because it is always a best practice to not store sensitive information in the heap (our variables are all young generation and will be garbaged after the method call).

Having retrieved the username and password, we can now call the legacy system as shown in the following code:

```
if (userName != null && password != null && userName.length() > 0 &&
password.length() > 0)
{
        checkUsernameAndPassword(userName, password);
    } else {
        throw new LoginException("username and/or password cannot be
null");
    }
```

We launch `LoginException` if our necessary credentials are null or if the SSO system cannot validate our user. If everything is right we can declare a successful login and save our principals for later use, as shown in the following code snippet:

```
    loginSucceeded = true;

    principalsForSubject.add(new WLSUserImpl(userName));
    principalsForSubject.add(new WLSGroupImpl("Packt"));

    return loginSucceeded;
}
```

Here `principalsForSubject` and `loginSucceeded` are two fields declared in the following manner:

```
private boolean loginSucceeded;
private List<Principal> principalsForSubject = new
ArrayList<Principal>();
```

Lifecycle methods – commit(), abort(), and logout()

Now, we need to implement the remaining `commit`, `abort`, and `logout` methods, taking care of the behavior expected by the client of the `LoginModule` interface (you can read more about this at `http://docs.oracle.com/javase/6/docs/technotes/guides/security/jaas/JAASLMDevGuide.html#commit`).

The expected external behavior for the `commit` method is as follows:

login()/commit()	Success	Failure
Success	return `true`	throw exception
Failure	return `false`	return `false`

We saved the result of the `login()` method in `loginSucceeded`. We must always return `false` in case of a failed login and return `true` otherwise (this simple method can't fail in the case of a successful login, so we remove `throw LoginException` from the method signature), as shown in the following code snippet:

```
@Override
public boolean commit() {
    LOGGER.info("PacktLoginModuleImpl.commit");
    if (loginSucceeded) {
        subject.getPrincipals().addAll(principalsForSubject);
        principalsInSubject = true;
        return true;
    } else {
        return false;
    }
}
```

We need to save the fact that the `commit` method was successful in the `principalsInSubject` local field so that we can react appropriately in case of of `abort()`.

For the `abort()` method we must distinguish when it's called after a successful login, as shown in the following table:

commit()/abort()	Success	Failure
Success	return `true`	throw exception
Failure	return `true`	throw exception

Or after an unsuccessful login, as follows:

commit()/abort()	Success	Failure
Success	return `false`	return `false`
Failure	return `false`	return `false`

The following code shows a simple implementation considering that abort() itself can't fail:

```
@Override
public boolean abort() {
    LOGGER.info("PacktLoginModuleImpl.abort");
    if( !loginSucceeded ) {
      return false;
    }
    if (principalsInSubject) {
        subject.getPrincipals().
        removeAll(principalsForSubject);
        principalsInSubject = false;
    }
    return true;
}
```

Finally, we need to implement logout() as shown in the following code snippet:

```
@Override
public boolean logout() throws LoginException {
  LOGGER.info("PacktLoginModuleImpl.logout");
  if( principalsInSubject ) {
    if( !subject.isReadOnly() ) {
      subject.getPrincipals().removeAll(principalsForSubject);
    } else {
      for(Principal principal: principalsForSubject ) {
        if( principal instanceof Destroyable ) {
          try {
            ((Destroyable)principal).destroy();
          } catch (DestroyFailedException e) {
            LOGGER. throwing("PacktLoginModuleImpl", "logout", e);
            throw new LoginException("cannot destroy principal " +
principal.getName());
          }
        } else {
          throw new LoginException("cannot destroy principal
"+principal.getName());
        }
      }
    }
  }
  return true;
}
```

As we can see in the previous code, the implementation must remove or destroy the principals inside the associated `Subject` objects that were created by this `LoginModule`, while taking care not to touch any principals added by other modules, and eventually signaling its failure of clearing them with a `LoginException` exception.

We can do a clean-install again now and then our Authentication Provider is ready for use.

A simple SSO JSP

Before we can run our Provider, we need to emulate the legacy SSO system. We do this now with a simple JSP, as shown in the following code snippet:

```
<%@ page contentType="text/plain;charset=UTF-8" language="java" %><%
    if( "testuser".equals(request.getParameter("username")) &&
  "testpassword".equals(request.getParameter("password"))) {
        response.setStatus(200);
    } else {
        response.setStatus(401);
    }
%>
```

For this example, we can deploy it inside the `webapps/ROOT` folder of any Tomcat server running on port **8080**. In case you use another port (or to add a context-path), the `authentication.services.url` property must be updated.

Running the provider

We can now run the provider calling the servlet that we wrote in the `chapter3-web` folder by using `http://localhost:7001/chapter3-web/myprotectedresource`.

We will be asked for the username and password, and after entering `testuser` and `testpassword` respectively we will receive an error telling us that the current user does not have enough privileges to execute the EJB method. The following error message will be displayed:

```
[EJB:010160]Security violation: User testuser has insufficient
permission to access EJB type=<ejb>, application=chapter3-ear,
module=/chapter3-web, ejb=NoInterfaceBeanInWarModule, method=echo,
methodInterface=Local, signature={java.lang.String}.
```

This is not an error but a desired effect; it is just that our `testuser` is not entitled to call the EJB method. In case you want to see an execution working well you can simply comment out the execution of the EJB in the servlet, as shown in the following code:

```
//resp.getWriter().println("echo:"+service.echo("echo"));
```

Alternatively, modify the EJB so that this user is powerful enough to execute it. It is a good exercise to map a new role to the group that is associated with this user.

If now we look at the WebLogic's log, we can see that our lifecycle methods have been correctly called in the order we expected:

```
INFO: PacktLoginModuleImpl.initialize
INFO: PacktLoginModuleImpl.login
INFO: PacktLoginModuleImpl.commit
```

Summary

In this chapter we learned how to code an Authentication Provider using Maven and JAAS technology, from scratch—starting from the creation of the project, to the understanding of the MDF file, to the writing of the necessary code. With this knowledge, you can also write a custom Identity Asserter or Credential Mapping Provider; you only need to change the MDF file and the interface implemented by the Provider class.

5
Integrating with Kerberos SPNEGO Identity Assertion

This chapter covers the configurations and requirements needed to implement the **Single Sign-On (SSO)** authentication process with SPNEGO in your infrastructure. This chapter covers the following topics:

- Using Identity Assertion SSO Kerberos in a Microsoft domain
- SPNEGO Identity Assertion configuration

Using Identity Assertion SSO Kerberos in a Microsoft domain

Identity Assertion is a provider mechanism that permits users to trust your identity using a token stored in your machine, by the **Simple and Protected Negotiation Mechanism (SPNEGO)**. Here, your identity is exchanged with the server by HTTP transaction in silent mode (Single Sign-On) without entering the username and password.

You can use these pages to implement your security in a preexisting context using a predefined structured architecture with users and groups.

In our case, we will analyze a SPNEGO Single Sign-On configuration in a Microsoft domain context using the Kerberos native token and Oracle JRockit JVM embedded with WebLogic Server.

WebLogic Server supports Kerberos tokens even if you install it in a server that is not Microsoft OS-based, for example, Linux OS. This is because the trust relationship will be done by the Oracle WebLogic Server security layer and not by the Operating System.

Windows client needs to be in the Active Directory domain

Before we go on, we need to check if your machine is part of an Active Directory domain and check the correct configuration in your computer properties. If you can see your Windows domain name in the **Domain** section, you're a member. Otherwise, your computer needs to be synced with your target configuration domain by the administrator.

Windows client session needs to be logged in the Active Directory domain

On your client's Windows machine, the login phase in the domain generates a valid Kerberos token cached with your credentials; you can check if the token is generated correctly with some powerful tools, which are very useful during diagnostic sessions.

You can find these utilities on the **Windows Server 2003 Resource Kit Tools** package and you can download this from the Microsoft site at `http://www.microsoft.com/en-us/download/details.aspx?id=17657`.

Kerbtray is a graphical and easy-to-use Microsoft tool that will display a detailed list of your Kerberos tokens cached with some key information:

- Service name: Your configured service principal name
- Valid ticket time: Expiration date and time
- Encryption type: Type of encryption supported

You can also use this tool to clean your local token cache by right-clicking on the tray icon and selecting the **Purge tickets** option.

Klist is a command-line utility that will permit you to view and clean your local token caches; with this command you can easily write a batch command to pilot or monitor your token cache for a long time.

The following command redirects the output to a file, to save your token status:

```
klist > c:\token.list.txt
```

Integrated Windows Authentication

It's very important to check if this client browser setting is enabled; without this, the Single Sign-On process will not work.

To check your settings, right-click on the Internet Explorer icon in your desktop and select **Properties**. Go to the **Advanced** tab and scroll down to the **Security** section and check **Enable Integrated Windows Authentication**—if it's not already selected.

> **Restarting the Internet Explorer browser**
>
> If you are using a proxy server, be sure your local domain names are in the exceptions field; this permits a direct connection from client to server without passing over a proxy server and preserves your sent token.

DNS URL entry configuration and SPN definition

It's essential to register a DNS record that will be used to access your Single Sign-On application installed in the WebLogic Server instance.

It's advisable to register all hostnames in your scenario—WebLogic nodes (for example, a network load balancer device), web server nodes, and any other existing and associated virtual IP. This information will allow us to register all **Service Principal Names** (**SPNs**), which are enabled to mark a trusted Single Sign-On access in your application at any level. This is powerful when you need to troubleshoot a problem.

The DNS entry can be provided with the internal Active Directory DNS service, or externally with some appliance DNS Server or some standard-compliant DNS Server. The working of the entire process is shown in the following diagram:

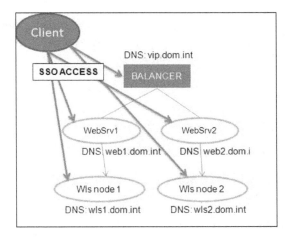

Technical Active Directory user

On the Active Directory side we need to create a technical user to associate the Service Principal Name; this technical user is fundamental in the token verification phase.

Add a sample user by checking the **User cannot change password** and **Password never expires** checkboxes (leave any other settings to default values). Check the **Use Kerberos DES encryption types for this account** option under the **Account** tab.

[Check this option only if you are using Active Directory running on Windows Server 2003.]

If you are using JVM 6 (or a later version) and Windows Server 2008, don't check this option; by doing so we can configure the encryption method as RC4 HMAC. This encryption type doesn't need any other Active Directory technical user configuration.

Also consider that Oracle certifies Internet Explorer 8.0 and FireFox 7.0.1 clients—which access user accounts defined in Active Directory and are encrypted with the AES-128, AES-256, or RC4 types—will run on a Windows 7 Enterprise platform.

Change the user password and remember it. If you change the encryption type, reset the user password again.

Now we need to add our Service Principal Name on this user; to access it we must use an Active Directory privileged user, as they can edit services to our technical user.

For example, consider the URL `http://wls1.dom.int`, which points to the IP configured on your WebLogic Server instance. Open a DOS command with a privileged user on a Windows machine in the domain and enter the following command:

```
setspn -A HTTP/wls1 technicaluser
```

The previous command associates the URL of WebLogic Server to our user.

```
setspn -A HTTP/wls1.dom.int technicaluser
```

The previous command associates the URL of WebLogic Server with the full domain specified to our user.

In this way, you have enabled the `http://wls1.dom.int` URL (and only that) to accept a Kerberos session and register any other URLs.

To check your registered Service Principal Name user entry, use the following command:

```
setspn -L technicaluser
```

Some important rules while creating a technical user with Active Directory are as follows:

- Create the DNS entry before configuring your Service Principal Name
- Don't associate the same Service Principal Name record to more than one technical user
- Don't define any TCP ports in the Service Principal Name; a single record can cover any port
- Any Service Principal Name changes need to follow the Keytab generation phase again (explained in the next section)

Keytab generation and the krb5 config file

Before proceeding we need to have a local Kerberos configuration file in accordance with your Active Directory and Kerberos configuration.

Check under `${java.home}/lib/security/krb5.conf` or `%windir%\krb5.ini`.

This file contains a list of important parameters; the following code snippet shows a sample section from that file:

```
[libdefaults]
   default_realm = DOM.INT
  ticket_lifetime=600
   default_tkt_enctypes = rc4-hmac aes128-cts des3-cbc-sha1 des-cbc-md5
des-cbc-crc
   default_tgs_enctypes = rc4-hmac aes128-cts des3-cbc-sha1 des-cbc-md5
des-cbc-crc
   permitted_enctypes = rc4-hmac aes128-cts des3-cbc-sha1 des-cbc-md5
des-cbc-crc
[realms]
  LOCAL.DOM.INT = {
     kdc = dc0.local.dom.int:88
     default_domain= DOM.INT
  }
[domain_realm]
   .dom.int = DOM.INT
[appdefaults]
autologin = true
```

```
forward = true
forwardable = true
encrypt = true
```

On a Windows machine in the domain with a JDK installation (it is better to use the same JDK version that is installed on the server side), use the following command in a DOS window to generate a Keytab file:

```
c:\Programs\jdk1.6.0_02\bin\Ktab.exe -a technicaluser pwduser -k
keytabname.keytab
```

With this, the following output is displayed:

```
Done!
Service key for technicaluser is saved in c:\Programs\jdk1.6.0_02\bin\
jdk1.6.0_02\bin\keytabname.keytab
```

To check your Keytab file use the following command:

```
c:\Programs\jdk1.6.0_02\bin\klist.exe -e -f -t -K -k c:\Programs\
jdk1.6.0_02\bin\jdk1.6.0_02\bin\keytabname.keytab
```

The following output will be displayed in the command-line window:

```
Key tab: c:\test.keytab, 5 entries found.
[1] Service principal: technicaluser@DOM.INT
        KVNO: 1
        Key type: 17
        Key: 0x8818f354b7c348bf234b95caffa9cdd
        Time stamp: May 11, 2012 11:57
[2] Service principal: technicaluser@DOM.INT
        KVNO: 1
        Key type: 16
        Key: 0xec4f8cd12342223a2423425d7fa4e9fd
        Time stamp: May 11, 2012 11:57
[3] Service principal: technicaluser@DOM.INT
        KVNO: 1
        Key type: 23
        Key: 0xd18a478dfcc5a1d2342311ac23165fa
        Time stamp: May 11, 2012 11:57
[4] Service principal: technicaluser@DOM.INT
        KVNO: 1
        Key type: 3
```

```
Key: 0x31d3b33132412222cfghb3e

Time stamp: May 11, 2012 11:57
```

[5] Service principal: technicaluser@DOM.INT

```
KVNO: 1

Key type: 1

Key: 0x31d3b123412tffgb0cb3e

Time stamp: May 11, 2012 11:57
```

Move the generated Keytab file and copy the `krb5.ini` file—now renamed to `krb5.conf` in the WebLogic Server—to the home WebLogic domain folder.

krb5.conf keytabname.keytab

This file, on the server side, needs to be both readable and accessible to the user that starts the WebLogic Server.

When on your server you use a JVM with a version greater than 1.6 update 21, keep in mind that now a new security control has been introduced.

In few words the KVNO number is checked and this is increased everytime you change your password on the KRDC. When this number doesn't match the one that we have on the keytab an exception is raised.

We have the following two solutions to solve this problem:

1. Disable this check setting the KVNO number to zero (using the `ktpass` command).

2. Retrieve the correct KVNO number with the "kvno" utility and then launch keytab the exact number of time to let the number increase to the same level.

JAAS file creation

This is another important file that tells the WebLogic Server to use the Kerberos login module, where the keytab files are located, and also the path of the technical user, with the associated Service Principal Name.

Edit a file named `krb5Login.conf` and copy that in the WebLogic Server in the WebLogic domain home folder.

Next, a sample configuration wherein your WebLogic Server uses Oracle JVM version 6 or higher is shown in the following code snippet:

```
com.sun.security.jgss.krb5.initiate {
```

```
        com.sun.security.auth.module.Krb5LoginModule required
        principal="technicaluser@DOM.INT" useKeyTab="true"
        keyTab="keytabname.keytab" storeKey="true" debug="false";
};
com.sun.security.jgss.krb5.accept {
        com.sun.security.auth.module.Krb5LoginModule required
        principal="technicaluser@DOM.INT" useKeyTab="true"
        keyTab="keytabname.keytab" storeKey="true" debug="false";
};
```

krb5Login.conf

This file on the server side needs be both readable and accessible to the user that starts the WebLogic Server.

WLS init startup arguments configuration

To activate our Kerberos configuration we need to specify some specific startup arguments; open WebLogic Admin Console and go to **Server | Start Arguments**. Then add the following:

```
-Djava.security.auth.login.config=krb5Login.conf
-Djavax.security.auth.useSubjectCredsOnly=false
-Dsun.security.krb5.debug=false
-Dweblogic.security.enableNegotiate=true
-Djava.security.krb5.conf=krb5.conf
-Dweblogic.wsee.component.exception=false
-DDebugSecurityAdjudicator=false
```

After this modification you need to restart your WebLogic server node; if you have multiple nodes in your cluster you need to apply these parameters for each one of them.

SPNEGO Identity asserter configuration

To find SPNEGO Identity Assertion, go to the Admin Console and select **Security Realms | myrealm | Providers**.

Click on the **Lock & Edit** button to lock and edit your domain, proceed to the **New** button (naming your provider with a personal reference), and select the **Negotiate Identity Assertion** provider from the list and click on **Ok**. Reorder the provider sequence on top after LDAP is configured (see *Chapter 2, WebLogic Security Realm*). After all these modifications, restart all the nodes of your WebLogic Server, along with the Admin Console, to make your changes effective.

Now your WebLogic Server is able to accept Kerberos tokens in an HTTP connection, and it can establish a trusted relationship with your client when a Service Principal Name is called and the security is enabled in your Java application (refer to *Chapter 3, Java EE Security With WebLogic*, of this book to secure your path).

In the following diagram you can see an authentication schematic datasheet about the interaction actors:

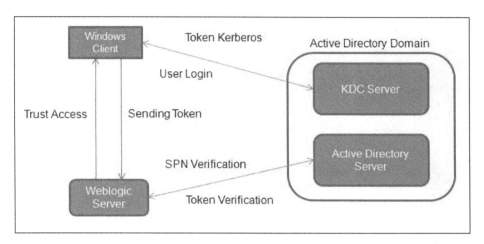

Debugging issues

If you receive any error message in the WebLogic log or if you just receive a Basic authentication form when you are trying to access a protected application resource, you probably have a configuration issue.

In the first instance, you can preserve your production configuration without touching it and try to do a client-side analysis with a network sniffer, for example, Wireshark. You will need to check if your Kerberos token is sent. Filter your network traffic for KRB5 protocols and by using the TCP port 88 (default TCP port to communicate with the Kerberos domain controller), you will be looking for some **Ticket Granting Server** (**TGS**) transactions. If you can't find any trace of these kinds of packages you need to move your debug on the server side or follow our previous configuration again, step-by-step.

To debug your server configuration, you need to increase your log verbosity using some debug switches in your WebLogic Server node's parameter using the console path. We can do this by first going to the **Servers** (your server name) option and then selecting **Debug | WebLogic | Security** and then choosing the **atn** (authentication) and the **atz** (authorization) options.

Check these options, click Enable, and then apply your changes.

Now we need to change some parameters to activate the maximum verbosity for the security layer, as explained in the following steps:

1. Edit your krb5Login.conf file and switch the following parameter to true:

    debug=true

2. Under the WebLogic Admin Console, on every server node that you want to debug, in the startup arguments you need to change your debug parameters to true, as follows:

    -Dsun.security.krb5.debug=true
    -DDebugSecurityAdjudicator=true

3. After this reconfiguration, you need to restart your WebLogic server nodes and analyze your server logs.

 This debug configuration creates very large log files; so please take care, the space usage can increase rapidly.

Summary

This chapter is a configuration guide to understand how the transparent authentication login process works (Single Sign-On), and what configurations are needed in your WebLogic Server to integrate with a Microsoft Active Directory Kerberos infrastructure.

We have focused on the key steps to follow for activating security access in your web application resources in a fast and easy way.

Index

Symbols

A

B

C

D

E

L

Lightweight Directory Access Protocol
(LDAP) 7
local LDAP server
  configuring 17
localRepository element 34
LoginContext class 7
login() method 7, 64-66
LoginModule
  abort method 65-67
  about 7, 53, 63
  code 63
  commit method 65-67
  lifecycle methods 65-67
  login() method 64, 65
  logout method 65-67
LoginModule interface 10
logout() method 67

M

mave-antrun-plugin 53
Maven
  plugins, reconfiguring 50-53
  URL 31
maven-antrun-plugin 48
maven-archetype-plugin
  used, for creating modules 31-33
maven-install-plugin 48, 51
maven-jar-plugin 48, 51
Maven plugins
  reconfiguring 50-53
Maven project
  about 47
  creating 48
  dependencies 49, 50
maven-resources-plugin 55
MBean
  about 11
  and JAAS 11
  defining, with MDF file 56-59
MBean Definition File (MDF) 10
MBeanImplBeanInfo class 59
MBean implementation
  authentication provider, implementing 62
  authentication provider, initializing 61
  writing 59, 60

MBeanMaker tool about 10, 11, 48
MBeans 8, 10
MBeanServer interface 10
MBean type 48
MDF file
  MBean, defining with 56-59
Microsoft Domain
  Identity Assertion SSO Kerberos, using in
    71
modules
  creating, with maven-archetype-plugin
    31-33
Multipart Authentication Provider 12
MXBean interface 10
MyProtectedServlet class 43

P

PacktAuthProviderImpl class 60
PacktLoginModuleImpl class 63
PasswordCredential interface 13
performance options 27
Perimeter Authentication 12
pom.xml file 35
Principal Validator Cache option 28
programmatic security
  about 42
  with WebLogic XACML Provider 42
Project Object Model (POM)
  about 31
  WebLogic MBeanMaker, adding to 53-56
ProviderClassName attribute 58
Purge tickets option 72

R

reconfiguring
  Maven plugins 50-53
resources, WebLogic 8
RunAs annotation
  about 45
  used, for modifying security identity 45

S

security 5
security concepts, Java EE 5, 6
SecurityContext interface 13

Thank you for buying
Securing WebLogic Server 12c

About Packt Publishing

Packt, pronounced 'packed', published its first book "Mastering phpMyAdmin for Effective MySQL Management" in April 2004 and subsequently continued to specialize in publishing highly focused books on specific technologies and solutions.

Our books and publications share the experiences of your fellow IT professionals in adapting and customizing today's systems, applications, and frameworks. Our solution based books give you the knowledge and power to customize the software and technologies you're using to get the job done. Packt books are more specific and less general than the IT books you have seen in the past. Our unique business model allows us to bring you more focused information, giving you more of what you need to know, and less of what you don't.

Packt is a modern, yet unique publishing company, which focuses on producing quality, cutting-edge books for communities of developers, administrators, and newbies alike. For more information, please visit our website: www.packtpub.com.

About Packt Enterprise

In 2010, Packt launched two new brands, Packt Enterprise and Packt Open Source, in order to continue its focus on specialization. This book is part of the Packt Enterprise brand, home to books published on enterprise software – software created by major vendors, including (but not limited to) IBM, Microsoft and Oracle, often for use in other corporations. Its titles will offer information relevant to a range of users of this software, including administrators, developers, architects, and end users.

Writing for Packt

We welcome all inquiries from people who are interested in authoring. Book proposals should be sent to author@packtpub.com. If your book idea is still at an early stage and you would like to discuss it first before writing a formal book proposal, contact us; one of our commissioning editors will get in touch with you.

We're not just looking for published authors; if you have strong technical skills but no writing experience, our experienced editors can help you develop a writing career, or simply get some additional reward for your expertise.

Advanced Penetration Testing for Highly-Secured Environments: The Ultimate Security Guide

ISBN: 978-1-84951-774-4   Paperback: 414 pages

Learn to perform professional penetration testing for highly-secured environments with this intensive hands-on guide

1. Learn how to perform an efficient, organized, and effective penetration test from start to finish

2. Gain hands-on penetration testing experience by building and testing a virtual lab environment that includes commonly found security measures such as IDS and firewalls

3. Take the challenge and perform a virtual penetration test against a fictional corporation from start to finish and then verify your results by walking through step-by-step solutions

WordPress 3 Ultimate Security

ISBN: 978-1-84951-210-7   Paperback: 408 pages

Protect your WordPress site and its network

1. Know the risks, think like a hacker, use their toolkit, find problems first – and kick attacks into touch

2. Lock down your entire network from the local PC and web connection to the server and WordPress itself

3. Find out how to back up and secure your content and, when it's scraped, know what to do to enforce your copyright

Please check **www.PacktPub.com** for information on our titles

Java EE 6 Cookbook for Securing, Tuning, and Extending Enterprise Applications

Packed with comprehensive recipes to secure, tune, and extend your Java EE applications

Mick Knutson

Java EE 6 Cookbook for Securing, Tuning, and Extending Enterprise Applications

ISBN: 978-1-84968-316-6   Paperback: 356 pages

Packed with comprehensive recipes to secure, tune, and extend your Java EE applications

1. Secure your Java applications using Java EE built-in features as well as the well-known Spring Security framework

2. Utilize related recipes for testing various Java EE technologies including JPA, EJB, JSF, and Web services

3. Explore various ways to extend a Java EE environment with the use of additional dynamic languages as well as frameworks

Metasploit Penetration Testing Cookbook

Over 70 recipes to master the most widely used penetration testing framework

Abhinav Singh

Metasploit Penetration Testing Cookbook

ISBN: 978-1-84951-742-3   Paperback: 268 pages

Over 70 recipes to master the most widely used penetration testing framework

1. More than 80 recipes/practical tasks that will escalate the reader's knowledge from beginner to an advanced level

2. Special focus on the latest operating systems, exploits, and penetration testing techniques

3. Detailed analysis of third party tools based on the Metasploit framework to enhance the penetration testing experience

Please check **www.PacktPub.com** for information on our titles

www.ingramcontent.com/pod-product-compliance
Lightning Source LLC
LaVergne TN
LVHW080102070326
832902LV00014B/2371